COTTAGE
COMFORT

Country-cottage style decorating, entertaining,
gardening, and quilting inspirations
for creating all the comforts of home

Lynette Jensen

LANDAUER BOOKS

This book was designed, produced, and published by Landauer Books
A division of Landauer Corporation
12251 Maffitt Road, Cumming, Iowa 50061

President: Jeramy Lanigan Landauer
Vice President: Becky Johnston
Managing Editor: Marlene Hemberger Heuertz
Art Director: Laurel Albright
Creative Director: Lynette Jensen
Photographer: Craig Anderson
Photostyling: Lynette Jensen and Margaret Sindelar
Technical Writer: Sue Bahr
Graphic Technician: Stewart Cott
Technical Illustrator: Lisa Kirchoff

We also wish to thank the support staff of the Thimbleberries® Design Studio:
Sherry Husske, Virginia Brodd, Renae Ashwill, Ardelle Paulson, Kathy Lobeck,
Carla Plowman, Julie Jergens, Pearl Baysinger, Tracy Schrantz, Leone Rusch, and Julie Borg.

Library of Congress Cataloging-in-Publication Data

Jensen, Lynette.
Cottage comfort : country-cottage style decorating, entertaining,
gardening, and quilting inspirations for creating all the comforts of home/by Lynette Jensen.
p. cm.
Cover title: Thimbleberries classic country.
ISBN 1-890621-19-6
1. Textile crafts. 2. Decoration and ornament, Rustic. 3. Interior decoration--Amateurs' manuals.
4. Entertaining. I. Title: Thimbleberries classic country. II. Thimbleberries, Inc. III. Title.

TT699 .J46 2001
747--dc21   00-067820

contents

Foreword

When our daughter married, my husband Neil and I became empty nesters and Kerry and Trevor became early nesters. Our son, Matthew, had already left home to launch his career in the "big city."

After 33 years of marriage, Neil and I found ourselves with more room and furnishings than needed.

In contrast, Trevor who after graduation from college was working via computer from a home office, and Kerry who had completed law school, were about to move into their "empty" starter home and needed help. As with most young couples just starting out, their goal was to furnish a home on a limited budget. Carrying on a family tradition, it seemed the right time to pass down treasured pieces to the next generation.

As we moved dressers, cupboards, chairs, and tables from our home to theirs, it was the perfect opportunity to create a decorating scheme using today's fashion colors as accents for the old-fashioned favorite furnishings. After all the scrubbing, painting, stenciling, and upholstering, it was fun to stand back and admire the transformation from house to home.

On the following pages, treat yourself to a decorating-dream tour of Trevor and Kerry Jensen-Olson's warm and inviting "new" old home, and join with me in a toast to their continued happiness in the cottage of their dreams!

Lynette Jensen

Introduction to
Cottage Comfort

With roots firmly planted in the soil of the English countryside, cottage-style rooms burst into bloom—in bright contrast to England's gray skies and cloudy days. Past generations discovered how to chase away the gloom by surrounding their tiny cottages with an abundance of flowers and then transforming them into veritable indoor gardens brimming with cascades of floral bouquets printed on cheery cotton chintz. Meeting the challenges of limited budgets, they mixed and matched the old with the new by painting, stenciling, and slip-covering. For many of us, just the mention of "cottage" evokes memories of simpler times. With today's emphasis on casual country-cottage style decorating and entertaining, returning to the pleasures of the past is as easy as coming home.

On the following pages designer and teacher Lynette Jensen shares her secrets for creating your own safe haven filled with soul-satisfying comforts. Since simplicity is at the heart of cottage-style decorating, most of what you'll need is right at hand. With a little imagination and Lynette's easy-to-follow directions, tips, and touches, you'll soon surround yourself with the serenity you've been seeking. Lynette shows you how to cultivate garden-inspired themes throughout your home by combining old furniture, dried flowers, and vintage fabrics with your favorite keepsakes and collectibles.

If you're an early-nester, an empty-nester, or somewhere in between, and regardless of whether your home is the size of a cottage or a castle, this book is for you. Now is the perfect time to incorporate Lynette's budget-pleasing, garden-inspired, small-scale decorating, entertaining, and quilting inspirations into your current lifestyle. After all, creating intimate and inviting ambience by blending the old with the new is the essence of country-cottage style!

Discover a new neutral color. In the living room shown below, sage sets the stage for country-cottage style decorating throughout Kerry and Trevor's home. This enduring shade of green is mellow, rich, and restful and coordinates with almost all other colors as well as the standard-issue cream or beige. With sage lending depth and character to the walls, colorful accents of yellow and cream warmed up with splashes of red share the scene.

In the corner, a screen made from discarded shutters removed from Lynette and Neil's home during a renovation seven years ago, provides a textured backdrop for a corner display of quilt and collectibles. And at left, an old painted pine table serves as a coffee table and nesting place for a pair of children's library chairs parked across from the sofa (shown on page 26) upholstered in sunshine yellow and poppy red.

Carry the color throughout the room.
Antique yellow and white plates are showcased
on a simple shelf made from window molding
salvaged from a small country school near the
town of Hutchinson, Minnesota, where Lynette
lives. The plate's matching sugar and creamer
rest atop a green wooden box with cream
drawers sharing space with a yellow pitcher and
an antique Shawnee ceramic teapot. This
grouping is softened by a dried arrangement of
pastel roses from Kerry's wedding bouquet.

The homemade buffet with drawers simply
fashioned from shipping crates was the first
antique piece Lynette purchased at an auction
for the magnificent sum of $10. It was badly in
need of repair, and her first "find" also became
her first refinishing project!

Find double-duty beauty. Long live wicker!
An antique wicker chair and rocker which once
belonged to Neil and Lynette, also happened to
be the first chairs in their living room.

As versatile as it is enduring, wicker works
just as well indoors or outdoors. For small-space
or budget decorating, chairs that double your
pleasure are truly a delight.

Over-sized ruffled pillows made from vintage-
style reproduction floral fabric are backed with
scraps from an antique woven bedspread dyed
sage green that adds valuable accents of color
and texture while costing next to nothing.

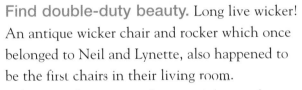

Group for greater impact.
The magic of "threes" comes to life in this trio of antique Easter postcards grouped for greater impact and framed as inexpensive art for the wall. Decorating touches include double matting of cream and sage, and selected postcards with vivid touches of the yellow and red accent colors already used for the room.

Below, the cream corner cut-work shelf contrasts with the sage wall and is home to a cream and floral teapot collection started for Kerry. Lynette finds it fun to hunt for additional pieces for the collection when she's at an auction or antique shop.

Create artful arrangements from flea market finds.
Lynette demonstrates that it doesn't have to be expensive to be artful.

At left, dried flowers from Kerry's wedding fill a vase that is similar in color to another vase of a complementary size and shape. To the right, two pitchers add height with an inexpensive antique platter on a plate easel displayed as a piece of ceramic floral art.

Brighten the corner. With small-space decorating, every inch counts. This handsome antique Scandinavian-styled pine hutch tucks beautifully into a corner of the small dining room separated from the living room only by an arch.

The hutch was a wedding gift to Kerry and Trevor from Neil and Lynette and is a treasure-house for storing and displaying Kerry's growing collection of teapots and teacups. The cups shown at left were passed down to Kerry from Neil's mother as a recent birthday gift.

On the wall above the dining table, antique water-color prints carry the yellow and cream accent colors throughout the combination dining and living room.

Take it from salvage to spectacular in no time at all. Creating a cozy family room need not be costly with old things used in new ways. Here, the fireplace mantel becomes a work of art with a few simple inspirations that go from salvage to spectacular.

Pussywillows and red-twigged dogwood branches in terra cotta vases painted cream fan out to frame an old basement window screen holding a bundle of dried flowers. Behind the screen, a salvaged tin ceiling panel mounted in a rustic wooden frame shows off a detailed embossing pattern. For best results, Lynette recommends using a latex paint in an eggshell finish, wiping off the excess to highlight the embossing.

Carry the earthy colors throughout the room by arranging autumn leaves and cattails in a ceramic vase nestled on a blanket-covered trunk.

Use old things new ways. As anyone can tell you, if comfort comes first in the family room, start with flannel quilts and the rest will follow. Keeping comfy quilts handy for daily use is a snap using a hall tree, an apple basket, and an antique hutch. The hall tree was first used by Kerry in her college dorm room, and the hutch belonged to Lynette's Grandma Geier and has been passed down from mother to daughter for four generations.

The large cupboard at left was originally built by Lynette's brother-in-law. Painted and distressed to look old, the cupboard is fitted with discarded window shutters and is deep enough to cleverly disguise the television set and other electronics.

Country cottage-style goes "corporate" in the home office. Yes, it is possible to make state of the art computer equipment feel right at home in a spare bedroom. However, it is imperative that the room be computer friendly and "feel" professional.

But as shown here, it is also friendly to the eye with masculine country accents scattered about. On the wall, a model sailboat lends an air of antiquity, along with the old metal truck used as a key and mail caddy.

Make a statement with varsity art. Instead of the traditional framed college diploma, show school spirit with framed and matted antique varsity letters. Kerry and Trevor met at St. Olaf College where Kerry played on the Women's Tennis Team and Trevor played football.

Other college-inspired decorative accents include the four framed black and white photographs taken by Kerry for a college photography class.

Spare doesn't have to be sparse.
A tiny spare bedroom can still seem spacious
even when filled to the brim. Lynette started
the pieced and stenciled May Basket Quilt 14
years ago and finished it as a gift for Kerry
and Trevor's first home. Stenciled muslin
borders frame the quilt center and the walls are
stenciled using a lighter shade of paint for the
vertical rows of stenciled floral stripes.

For the windows, ticking-striped fabric
valances top off vintage lace curtains for an
unfussy touch of softness.

Below, vintage floral prints on the wall
between the windows continue the color
scheme throughout the room.

Add a cupboard, not a closet. Even though
Kerry and Trevor reserve this room for guests, the
small closet was a storage challenge. Solving the
problem was a cinch with an old kitchen cupboard
painted yellow and stenciled with floral accents. It
holds extra quilts and linens, and offers plenty of
space for storing guest essentials such as towels,
scented soaps, and bath oils.

The trellis and dried florals in a postcard-trimmed
galvanized tin repeat the room's garden theme.
Lynette used an antique seed tin passed down from
Kerry's great-grandmother to display dried florals.
The tin has been decorated with antique postcards
(see page 76) and serves with the trellis to enhance
the room's garden theme.

Make room for memories and more.
Two bedrooms upstairs function differently. One serves as the master bedroom and the other as Kerry's private study/retreat.

In contrast to Trevor's home office, hers is a restful blend of keepsakes that evoke childhood memories. A pleasant place for writing or journaling, the scallop-backed desk stands ready with a vintage vase filled with pencils, and a pair of cast-iron book-ends holding favorite books. The vintage pieces are accented with an antique "yard-long" framed print. The tin basket holds special memories—dried flowers from Kerry and Trevor's wedding.

A "ladies" wing-back chair upholstered in a charming floral print with a miniature round ottoman to match, made Kerry's law-school studies a little more comfortable. Now, she uses it for relaxing after a long day at the law firm.

The ruffled pillow featuring an embroidered tennis player from the 1930s is a reminder of Kerry's many years spent playing tennis in high school and college.

The antique buggy shown below was purchased for Kerry when she was a little girl of three. It now functions quite nicely as a handy caddy for keeping a quilt nearby.

Small, but serene. When it comes to getting a good night's sleep, the size of the room is far less important than the ambiance it offers. The master bedroom, opposite, is small but mighty when it comes to peacefully blending all the elements that transcend the seasons. Stenciled autumn leaves on the wall color-coordinate with the rust and blue fabrics in the Patchwork Snowflake Quilt accented with floral pillows and shams in a variety of textures—flannel, linen, and calico.

By painting the second-hand dresser a similar color as the bedroom walls, Kerry made the dresser blend in and the room appear larger.

cottage Comforts

hemes for country-cottage style decorating can range from traditional to contemporary, but the key is keeping it casual. Whether you fill your home with priceless antiques or garage-sale finds, the finished feeling must be one of welcoming comfort.

Decorating for ease and style on a budget is surprisingly attainable with soft comforts that lend an air of romance and nostalgia to any room regardless of its size. Here and on the following pages, you'll find a variety of soft comforts that Lynette designed for small-space decorating like Kerry and Trevor's home, that work just as well in a larger setting.

Lynette began by creating a color palette of sage green with splashes of yellow and cream accented with occasional touches of red. Keeping the color scheme in mind, she then began collecting a variety of furnishings to mix and match throughout the house.

Kerry and Trevor's living room, shown opposite and on the previous page, is a great example of how easily it can all work together. For the corner detailed here, the sage-green walls are the backdrop for framed floral prints with fabric patchwork mats and vintage round floral pictures. Antique shutters are host to a multi-colored pieced quilt, and the cheerful yellow print on the sofa coordinates with the variety of fabrics used for the pillows.

Turn the page for little decorating ideas with big impact. Make these soft comforts in colors to coordinate with your decorating scheme to create your own interpretation of that bountiful look of country-cottage style.

blocks and blooms
Union Square Quilt

Big, bold blocks in bright colors blend with the delicate florals embroidered on the outer muslin triangles.

Fabrics & Supplies

Finished Size: 85-inches square

Yardage is based on 42-inch wide fabric

5-3/4 yards MUSLIN for blocks, side triangles, corner triangles, middle border, and outer border

1/3 yard each of 25 ASSORTED MEDIUM PRINTS for blocks

7/8 yard GREEN PRINT for narrow borders

3/4 yard MUSLIN for binding

7-1/2 yards BACKING FABRIC

QUILT BATTING, at least 89-inches square

Optional: Purchased embroidery patterns to transfer onto the muslin side triangles and embroidery floss.

Union Square Blocks Make 25 Blocks

Cutting

From each of the 25 ASSORTED MEDIUM PRINTS:

- Cut 1, 4-1/2 x 42-inch strip. From this strip cut:
  1, 4-1/2-inch square
  4, 2-1/2 x 4-1/2-inch rectangles
  2, 2-7/8-inch squares

- Cut 1, 2-1/2 x 42-inch strip. From this strip cut:
  16, 2-1/2-inch squares

From MUSLIN:

- Cut 35, 2-1/2 x 42-inch strips.
  From these strips cut:
  200, 2-1/2 x 4-1/2-inch rectangles
  200, 2-1/2-inch squares

- Cut 4, 2-7/8-inch x 42-inch strips.
  From these strips cut: 50, 2-7/8-inch squares

Piecing

For each Union Square block you will need eight
2-1/2 x 4-1/2-inch Muslin rectangles, eight 2-1/2-inch
Muslin squares, four 2-1/2-inch triangle-pieced squares,
and one set of Medium Print pieces (one 4-1/2-inch square, four
2-1/2 x 4-1/2-inch rectangles, and sixteen 2-1/2-inch squares).

Step 1   Position a 2-1/2-inch Medium Print square on the
corner of a 2-1/2 x 4-1/2-inch Muslin rectangle.
Draw a diagonal line on the Medium Print square, and
stitch on the line. Trim the seam allowance to 1/4-inch,
and press. Repeat this process at the opposite corner of
the Muslin rectangle. Make 8 units. Sew the units
together in pairs, and press. At this point each unit
should measure 4-1/2-inches square.

Make 8   Make 4

Step 2   Position a 2-1/2-inch Muslin square on the left-hand
corner of a 2-1/2 x 4-1/2-inch Medium Print rectangle.
Draw a diagonal line on the Muslin square, and stitch
on the line. Trim the seam allowance to 1/4-inch,
and press.

        Make 4

Step 3   With right sides together, layer a 2-7/8-inch Medium
Print square and a 2-7/8-inch Muslin square. Press
together, but do not sew. Cut the layered square in half
diagonally to make 2 sets of triangles. Stitch 1/4-inch

from the diagonal edge of the 2 pairs of triangles, and
press. Repeat this process with the remaining 2-7/8-inch
Medium Print and Muslin squares. Sew a 2-1/2-inch
Muslin square to the left edge of each triangle-pieced
square, and press. At this point each unit should measure
2-1/2 x 4-1/2-inches.

Make 4, 2-1/2-inch   Make 4
triangle-pieced squares

Step 4   Sew a Step 3 unit to the top
of a Step 2 unit, and press.
Make 4 units. At this point
each unit should measure
4-1/2-inches square.

Make 4

Step 5   Referring to the block diagram, sew a Step 1 unit to both
sides of the 4-1/2-inch Medium Print square, and press.
Sew a Step 4 unit to both sides of the remaining Step 1
units, and press. Sew the 3 horizontal rows together to
make a block. At this point the block should measure
12-1/2-inches square.

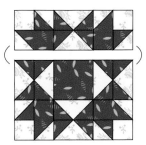

Step 6   Repeat Steps 1 through 5 to make a total of 25 Union
Square blocks.

Quilt Center

*Note: The side and corner triangles are larger than necessary
and will be trimmed before the borders are added.*

Cutting

From MUSLIN:

- Cut 2, 19 x 42-inch strips. From these strips cut:
  3, 19-inch squares. Cut the squares diagonally into quarters for
  a total of 12 side triangles.
  2, 10-inch squares. Cut the squares in half diagonally for a
  total of 4 corner triangles

Assembling the Quilt Center

Step 1   Referring to the quilt diagram, lay out the Union Square blocks and Muslin side triangles. Sew the pieces together in diagonal rows. Press the seam allowances in alternating directions by rows so the seams will fit snugly together with less bulk.

Step 2   Pin the rows at the block intersections and sew the rows together. Press the seam allowances in one direction.

Step 3   Sew the Muslin corner triangles to the quilt center, and press.

Step 4   Trim away the excess fabric from the side and corner triangles, taking care to allow a 1/4-inch seam allowance beyond the corners of each block. Refer to Trimming the Side and Corner Triangles on page 136.

Borders

Note: The yardage given allows for the border strips to be cut on the crosswise grain. Diagonally piece the strips as needed, referring to page 136 for Diagonal Piecing Instructions.

Cutting

From GREEN PRINT:

- Cut 16, 1-1/2 x 42-inch narrow border strips

From MUSLIN:

- Cut 8, 1-1/2 x 42-inch middle border strips

- Cut 9, 6 x 42-inch outer border strips

Attaching the Borders

Step 1   To attach the first 1-1/2-inch wide Green narrow border strips, refer to page 135 for Border Instructions.

Step 2   To attach the 1-1/2-inch wide Muslin middle border strips, refer to page 135 for Border Instructions.

Step 3   To attach the second 1-1/2-inch wide Green narrow border strips, refer to page 135 for Border Instructions.

Step 4   To attach the 6-inch wide Muslin outer border strips, refer to page 135 for Border Instructions.

Putting It All Together

- Cut the 7-1/2 yard length of backing fabric into thirds crosswise to form 3, 2-1/2 yard lengths. Refer to Finishing the Quilt on page 135 for complete instructions.

Binding

Cutting

From MUSLIN:

- Cut 9, 2-3/4 x 42-inch strips

Sew the binding to the quilt using a 3/8-inch seam allowance. This measurement will produce a 1/2-inch wide finished double binding. Refer to page 136 for Binding and Diagonal Piecing Instructions.

Union Square Quilt

Tennis Pillow

In the first half of this century, pre-printed embroidery panels were all the rage. The stitcheries worked up
quickly because most of the design was already colored in and the embroidery was added as a finishing touch.

Instructions

Pillow Front

Lynette used a charming embroidered panel for this pillow front which was trimmed to 18-1/2-inches square.

Pillow Ruffle

Cutting

From GREEN PRINT:
- Cut 5, 2-5/8 x 42-inch strips for inner ruffle

From PEACH PRINT:
- Cut 5, 3-5/8 x 42-inch strips for outer ruffle

Piecing and Attaching the Ruffle

Step 1 Diagonally piece the 2-5/8-inch wide Green Print strips together and diagonally piece the 3-5/8-inch wide Peach Print strips together, referring to page 136 for Diagonal Piecing Instructions.

Step 2 Aligning long edges, sew the Green and Peach strips together, and press. With right sides facing, sew the short raw edges together with a diagonal seam to make a continuous ruffle strip. Trim the seam allowance to 1/4-inch, and press.

Step 3 Fold the strip in half lengthwise, wrong sides together, and press. Divide the ruffle strip into 4 equal segments, and mark the quarter points with safety pins.

Step 4 To gather the ruffle, position a heavyweight thread (or 2 strands of regular weight sewing thread) 1/4-inch in from the raw edges of the folded ruffle strip. You will need a length of heavyweight thread 144-inches long. Secure one end of the thread by stitching across it. Zigzag-stitch over the thread all the way around the ruffle, taking care not to sew through it.

Step 5 With right sides together, pin the ruffle to the pillow front, matching the quarter points of the ruffle to corners of the pillow front. Pull up the gathering stitches until the ruffle fits the pillow front, taking care to allow fullness in the ruffle at each corner. Sew the ruffle to the pillow front, using a 1/4-inch seam allowance.

Pillow Back

Cutting

From GREEN PRINT:
- Cut 2, 18-1/2 x 22-inch rectangles

Assembling the Pillow Back

Step 1 With wrong sides together, fold the 2, 18-1/2 x 22-inch Green rectangles in half to form 2, 11 x 18-1/2-inch double-thick pillow back pieces. Overlap the 2 folded edges by about 4-inches so the pillow back measures 18-1/2-inches square, and pin. Stitch around the entire piece to create a single pillow back.

Step 2 With right sides together, layer the pillow back and the pillow front, and pin. The ruffle will be turned toward the center of the pillow at this time. Stitch around the outside edges using a 1/2-inch seam allowance.

Step 3 Trim the pillow back and corner seam allowances if needed. Turn the pillow right side out and fluff up the ruffle. Insert the pillow form through the back opening.

vintage embroidery and crochet
Basket Pillow

Several years ago, Lynette found this crocheted basket that her grandmother had started but never finished. She turned it into a project by combining it with scraps of embroidery resulting in a pillow for Kerry's home that holds a basket-full of memories!

Fabrics & Supplies

Finished Size: 18-inch pillow without ruffle

Yardage is based on 42-inch wide fabric

A variety of EMBROIDERED PIECES
for pillow front

A CROCHETED BASKET for pillow front

1-1/8 yards BLUE PRINT
for ruffle and pillow back

18-inch square PILLOW FORM

Pillow Front

To make the pillow front, Lynette sewed together a variety of embroidered pieces and then trimmed the piece to 18-1/2-inches square. She hand-tacked a crocheted basket to this pieced square to complete the pillow front.

Pillow Ruffle

Cutting

From BLUE PRINT:
• Cut 5, 3 x 42-inch strips

Attaching the Ruffle

Step 1   Diagonally piece the 3-inch wide Blue strips together to make a continuous ruffle strip, referring to page 136 for Diagonal Piecing Instructions.

Step 2   Fold the strip in half lengthwise, wrong sides together, and press. Divide the ruffle strip into 4 equal segments, and mark the quarter points with safety pins.

Step 3   To gather the ruffle, position a heavyweight thread (or 2 strands of regular weight sewing thread) 1/4-inch in from the raw edges of the folded ruffle.

Secure   Zigzag

Note: You will need a length of heavyweight thread 144-inches long. Secure one end of the thread by stitching across it. Zigzag-stitch over the thread all the way around the ruffle, taking care not to sew through it.

Step 4   With right sides together, pin the ruffle to the pillow front, matching the quarter points of the ruffle to the corners of the pillow front. Pull up the gathering stitches until the ruffle fits the pillow front, taking care to allow fullness in the ruffle at each corner. Sew the ruffle to the pillow front, using a scant 1/4-inch seam allowance.

Pillow Back

Cutting

From BLUE PRINT:
• Cut 2, 18-1/2 x 22-inch rectangles

Assembling the Pillow Back

Step 1   With wrong sides together, fold the 2, 18-1/2 x 22-inch Blue rectangles in half to form 2, 11 x 18-1/2-inch double-thick pillow back pieces. Overlap the 2 folded edges by about 4-inches so the pillow back measures 18-1/2-inches square, and pin. Stitch around the entire piece to create a single pillow back, using a scant 1/4-inch seam allowance.

Step 2   With right sides together, layer the pillow back and the pillow front, and pin. The ruffle will be turned toward the center of the pillow at this time. Stitch around the outside edges using a 3/8-inch seam allowance.

Overlap

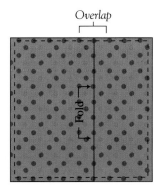

Fold

Step 3   Trim the pillow back and corner seam allowances if needed. Turn the pillow right side out and fluff up the ruffle. Insert the pillow form through the back opening.

springtime in bloom
May Basket Quilt

*A border of stenciled tulips
adds a touch of springtime
to the basket blocks.*

Fabrics & Supplies

Finished Size: 60 x 88-inches

Yardage is based on 42-inch wide fabric

5/8 yard ROSE PRINT for baskets

5/8 yard GREEN PRINT #1 for baskets

2-1/3 yards MUSLIN
for background and alternate blocks

1-1/4 yards MUSLIN or
COORDINATING FLORAL
PRINT for inner border (see option below*)

1-7/8 yards GREEN PRINT #2
for side and corner triangles, and outer border

1/4 yard GREEN FLORAL for corner squares

2/3 yard GREEN PRINT #2 for binding

5-1/4 yards BACKING FABRIC

QUILT BATTING, at least 64 x 92-inches

*Optional: Stencil from Stencil House,
Concord, NH (5-inch wide)
stencil paints, brush, and other supplies*

Note: Follow the fabric paint
manufacturer's instructions for stenciling on
fabric or use coordinating floral
print fabric for the inner border strips.

Instructions

Basket Blocks
Make 7 ROSE PRINT blocks
Make 8 GREEN PRINT #1 blocks

Note: As an option you could make all the basket blocks a different color.

Cutting

From ROSE PRINT:
- Cut 1, 6-7/8 x 42-inch strip
- Cut 3, 2-7/8 x 42-inch strips

From GREEN PRINT #1:
- Cut 1, 6-7/8 x 42-inch strip
- Cut 3, 2-7/8 x 42-inch strips

From MUSLIN:
- Cut 2, 6-7/8 x 42-inch strips
- Cut 6, 2-7/8 x 42-inch strips
- Cut 6, 2-1/2 x 42-inch strips. From these strips cut:
  30, 2-1/2 x 6-1/2-inch rectangles
  15, 2-1/2-inch squares

Piecing

Step 1   With right sides together, layer the 6-7/8 x 42-inch Rose strip and a 6-7/8 x 42-inch Muslin strip. Press together, but do not sew. Cut the layered strip into squares. Cut the layered squares in half diagonally to make 8 sets of triangles (you will be using only 7 sets of triangles). Stitch 1/4-inch from the diagonal edge of the 7 pairs of triangles, and press. At this point each triangle-pieced square should measure 6-1/2-inches square.

Crosscut 4, 6-7/8-inch squares

Make 7, 6-1/2-inch triangle-pieced squares

Step 2   In the same manner, with right sides together, layer the 2-7/8 x 42-inch Rose strips and 3 of the 2-7/8 x 42-inch Muslin strips in pairs. Press together, but do not sew. Cut the layered strips into squares. Cut the layered squares in half diagonally to make 63 sets of triangles. Stitch 1/4-inch from the diagonal edge of each pair of triangles, and press. At this point each triangle-pieced square should measure 2-1/2-inches square.

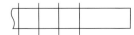

Crosscut 32, 2-7/8-inch squares

Make 63, 2-1/2-inch triangle-pieced squares

Step 3   Sew together 3 of the 2-1/2-inch triangle-pieced squares, and press. Referring to the Step 4 diagram, sew the units to the top edge of the 6-1/2-inch triangle-pieced squares, and press.

Make 7

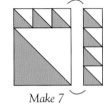

Make 7

Step 4   Sew together 4 of the 2-1/2-inch triangle-pieced squares, and press. Sew the units to the right edge of the 6-1/2-inch triangle-pieced squares, and press.

Step 5   Referring to the block assembly diagram for placement, sew a 2-1/2-inch triangle-pieced square to a 2-1/2 x 6-1/2-inch Muslin rectangle. Sew this unit to the left edge of the basket unit, and press. Sew a 2-1/2-inch triangle-pieced square to the left edge of a 2-1/2 x 6-1/2-inch Muslin rectangle, and press. Add a 2-1/2-inch Muslin square to the left edge of the unit, and press. Sew this unit to the bottom of the basket unit to complete the basket block, and press. At this point each basket block should measure 10-1/2-inches square.

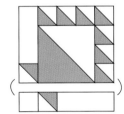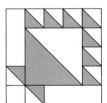

Make 7 Rose Basket Blocks

Step 6   In the same manner, make the Green baskets. With right sides together, layer the 6-7/8 x 42-inch Green strip and a 6-7/8 x 42-inch Muslin strip. Press together, but do not sew. Cut the layered strips into 4, 6-7/8-inch squares. Cut the layered squares in half diagonally to make 8 sets of triangles. Stitch 1/4-inch from the diagonal edge of each pair of triangles, and press. At this point each triangle-pieced square should measure 6-1/2-inches square.

Make 8, 6-1/2-inch triangle-pieced squares

Step 7   In the same manner, layer the 2-7/8 x 42-inch Green strips and 3 of the 2-7/8 x 42-inch Muslin strips in pairs. Press together, then cut the layered strips into 36, 2-7/8-inch squares. Cut the layered squares in half diagonally to make 72 sets of triangles. Stitch 1/4-inch from the diagonal edge of each pair of triangles, and press. At this point each triangle-pieced square should measure 2-1/2-inches square.

Make 72, 2-1/2-inch triangle-pieced squares

Step 8 Sew together 3 of the 2-1/2-inch triangle-pieced squares, and press. Referring to the block assembly diagram, sew the units to the top edge of the 6-1/2-inch triangle-pieced squares, and press.

Make 8

Step 9 Sew together 4 of the 2-1/2-inch triangle-pieced squares, and press. Referring to the block assembly diagram, sew the units to the right edge of the 6-1/2-inch triangle-pieced squares, and press.

Make 8

Step 10 Referring to the block assembly diagram for placement, sew a 2-1/2-inch triangle-pieced square to a 2-1/2 x 6-1/2-inch Muslin rectangle. Sew this unit to the left edge of the basket unit, and press. Sew a 2-1/2-inch triangle-pieced square to the left edge of a 2-1/2 x 6-1/2-inch Muslin rectangle, and press. Add a 2-1/2-inch Muslin square to the left edge of the unit, and press. Sew this unit to the bottom of the basket unit to complete the basket block, and press. At this point each basket block should measure 10-1/2-inches square.

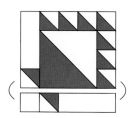 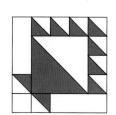

Make 8 Green Basket Blocks

Quilt Center

Note: The side and corner triangles are larger than necessary and will be trimmed before the borders are added.

Cutting

From MUSLIN:
- Cut 2, 10-1/2 x 42-inch strips.
  From these strips cut: 8, 10-1/2-inch squares

From GREEN PRINT #2:
- Cut 2, 17 x 42-inch strips. From these strips cut:
  3, 17-inch squares. Cut the squares diagonally into quarters for a total of 12 side triangles.
  2, 10-inch squares. Cut the squares in half diagonally for a total of 4 corner triangles.

Assembling the Quilt Center

Step 1 Referring to the quilt diagram, lay out the basket blocks, Muslin alternate blocks, and Green Print #2 side triangles. Sew the pieces together in diagonal rows. Press the seam allowances away from the basket blocks.

Step 2 Pin the rows at the block intersections and sew the rows together. Press the seam allowances in one direction.

Step 3 Sew the Green Print #2 corner triangles to the quilt center, and press.

Step 4 Trim away the excess fabric from the side and corner triangles, taking care to allow a 1/4-inch seam allowance beyond the corners of each block. Refer to Trimming Side and Corner Triangles on page 136.

Borders

Note: The yardage given allows for the border strips to be cut on the crosswise grain. Diagonally piece the strips as needed, referring to page 136 for Diagonal Piecing Instructions.

Cutting

From MUSLIN OR FLORAL PRINT:
- Cut 6, 6-1/2 x 42-inch inner border strips

From GREEN PRINT #2:
- Cut 8, 3-1/2 x 42-inch outer border strips

From GREEN FLORAL:
- Cut 4, 6-1/2-inch corner squares

Stenciling and Attaching the Borders

Step 1 Measure the quilt center from left to right and cut 2, 6-1/2-inch wide Muslin (or Floral Print) strips to that length. If using Muslin, center the stencil on each strip and stencil. After the paint has dried, sew the stenciled border strips to the top and bottom edges of the quilt, and press.

Step 2 Measure the quilt center from top to bottom including the seam allowances but not the borders just added. Cut 2, 6-1/2-inch wide Muslin (or Floral Print) strips to that length. If using Muslin, center the stencil on each strip and stencil. After the paint has dried, add the 6-1/2-inch Green Floral corner squares to both ends of the stenciled border strips. Sew the stenciled border strips to the side edges of the quilt, and press.

Step 3 To attach the 3-1/2-inch wide Green Print #2 outer border strips, refer to page 135 for Border Instructions.

Putting It All Together

Cut the 5-1/4 yard length of backing fabric in half crosswise to form 2 lengths at least 2-5/8 yards long. Refer to Finishing the Quilt on page 135 for complete instructions.

Binding

Sew the binding to the quilt using a 3/8-inch seam allowance. This measurement will produce a 1/2-inch wide finished double binding. Refer to page 136 for Binding and Diagonal Piecing Instructions.

From GREEN PRINT #2:
- Cut 8, 2-3/4 x 42-inch strips

May Basket Quilt

accent on color
Log Cabin Quilt

A red center square in the log cabin block adds a touch of accent color to this soft comfort that is right at home in any room of the house.

Fabrics & Supplies

Finished Size: 72 x 88-inches

Yardage is based on 42-inch wide fabric

5/8 yard RED PRINT for center squares

3/8 yard each of 12 ASSORTED DARK PRINTS for Log Cabin strips

5/8 yard each of 6 ASSORTED BEIGE to GOLD PRINTS for Log Cabin strips

3/4 yard RED PRINT for binding

5-1/4 yards BACKING FABRIC

QUILT BATTING, at least 76 x 94-inches

Instructions

Log Cabin Blocks Make 99 blocks
Cutting
From RED PRINT:

- Cut 7, 2-1/2 x 42-inch strips.
  From these strips cut: 99, 2-1/2-inch center squares

From each of the 12 ASSORTED DARK PRINTS:

- Cut 7, 1-1/2 x 42-inch strips

From each of the 6 ASSORTED BEIGE/GOLD PRINTS:

- Cut 13, 1-1/2 x 42-inch strips

Piecing
Note: You may vary the position of the Beige/Gold Print fabrics from block to block, or place them in the same position in each block. The same is true of the Assorted Dark Print fabrics. The fabrics in the quilt shown were varied to create a scrappy look.

Step 1 Sew a 1-1/2-inch wide Beige/Gold strip to a 2-1/2-inch Red square. Press the seam allowance toward the strip. Trim the strip even with the edges of the center square, creating a two-piece unit.

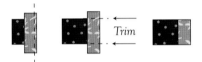

Step 2 Turn the two-piece unit a quarter turn to the left. Stitch a different 1-1/2-inch wide Beige/Gold strip to the two-piece unit. Press and trim the strip even with the edges of the two-piece unit.

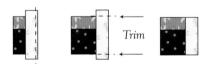

Step 3 Turn the unit a quarter turn to the left. Stitch a 1-1/2-inch wide Dark Print strip to the unit. Press and trim the strip even with the edges of the unit.

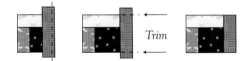

Step 4 Turn the unit a quarter turn to the left. Stitch a different 1-1/2-inch wide Dark Print strip to the unit. Press and trim the strip even with the edges of the unit.

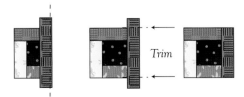

Step 5 Referring to the block diagram, continue adding 1-1/2-inch wide strips, alternating Beige/Gold strips and Dark Print strips to complete the Log Cabin block. Press each seam allowance toward the strip just added, and trim each strip before adding the next. Each Log Cabin block should measure 8-1/2-inches square when completed. Adjust the seam allowances if needed.

Make 99

Step 6 Repeat Steps 1 through 5 to make a total of 99 Log Cabin blocks.

Quilt Center

Step 1 Referring to the quilt diagram for placement, sew the Log Cabin blocks together in 11 rows of 9 blocks each. Press the seam allowances in alternating directions by rows so the seams will fit snugly together with less bulk.

Step 2 Pin the rows at the block intersections, and sew the rows together. Press the seam allowances in one direction.

Putting It All Together

Cut the 5-1/4 yard length of backing fabric in half crosswise to form 2, 2-5/8 yard lengths. Refer to Finishing the Quilt on page 135 for complete instructions.

Binding
Cutting
From RED PRINT:

- Cut 9, 2-3/4 x 42-inch strips

Sew the binding to the quilt using a 3/8-inch seam allowance. This measurement will produce a 1/2-inch wide finished double binding. Refer to page 136 for Binding and Diagonal Piecing Instructions.

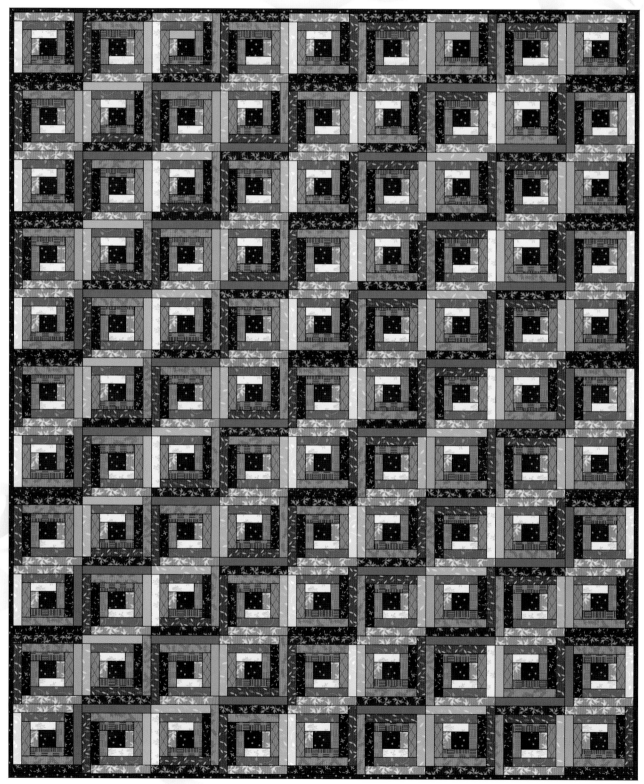

Log Cabin Quilt

trimmed to perfection
Block Pillowcase

Extended borders on pillowcases lend an air of abundance so vital to
creating cottage comfort. Here, a portion of the Union Square block is adapted to
fit the edge of the pillowcase which coordinates with the bed quilt.

Instructions

Fabrics & Supplies

Makes 1 Pillowcase

Yardage is based on 42-inch wide fabric

12-1/2-inch QUILT BLOCK (unfinished)

1-1/4 yards ROSE FLORAL
for pillow front, back, and cuff

1/8 yard GREEN PRINT for border

1/3 yard MUSLIN for cuff lining

19 x 29-inch BED PILLOW FORM

Union Square Block Pillowcase

Cutting

Cut an unfinished 12-1/2-inch quilt block in half diagonally to make 2 triangles.

From ROSE FLORAL:
- Cut 1, 29 x 41-inch rectangle for pillowcase
- Cut 1, 13-inch square cutting it in half diagonally to make 2 corner triangles
- Cut 1, 8-3/4 x 21-inch rectangle for cuff back

From GREEN:
- Cut 1, 1-1/2 x 41-1/2-inch border strip

From MUSLIN:
- Cut 1, 9-1/2 x 41-1/2-inch strip for cuff lining

Assembling the Pillow Trim

Step 1   Referring to the diagram, sew a Rose Floral corner triangle to both straight edges of the pieced triangle block, and press. Trim the unit to 8-3/4 x 21-inches.

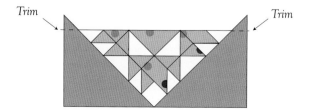

Trim   *Trim*

Step 2   With right sides together and raw edges aligned, sew the 8-3/4 x 21-inch Rose Floral cuff back rectangle to the left edge of the Step 1 unit, using a 1/2-inch seam allowance. Refer to the diagram below. Press the seam allowance open.

Step 3   With right sides together and raw edges aligned, sew the 1-1/2 x 41-1/2-inch Green border strip to the bottom edge of the Step 2 pieced cuff, using a 1/4-inch seam allowance. Press the seam allowance toward the Green border strip.

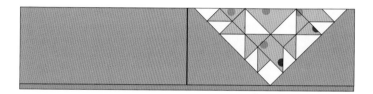

Step 4   With right sides together and long raw edges aligned, sew the 9-1/2 x 41-1/2-inch Muslin strip to the Green border edge of the Step 3 pieced cuff, using a 1/4-inch seam allowance. Press the Muslin lining to the back side of the pieced cuff and baste raw edges together.

Step 5   With right sides together and long raw edges aligned, sew the 29 x 41-1/2-inch Rose Floral rectangle to the basted raw edge of the Step 4 lined pieced cuff, using a 1/4-inch seam allowance. Press the seam allowance toward the Rose Floral rectangle.

Step 6   With the pieced cuff extended, right sides together and raw edges aligned, sew the side and bottom edges of the pillowcase, using a 1/2-inch seam allowance. Turn the pillowcase right side out and insert the pillow.

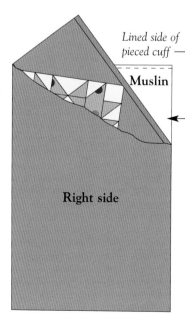

Lined side of pieced cuff

Muslin

Right side

a winter warmer
Patchwork
Snowflake Quilt

The snowflake blocks tumble to perfection on this warm and inviting quilt.

Fabrics & Supplies

Finished Size: 97 x 114-inches

Yardage is based on 42-inch wide fabric

7-1/4 yards BEIGE PRINT for blocks,
alternating blocks,
side triangles, and corner triangles

1/3 yard each of
30 ASSORTED DARK PRINTS for blocks

7/8 yard GOLD PRINT for inner border

1-5/8 yards GREEN FLORAL
for outer border

1 yard GREEN FLORAL for binding

8-5/8 yards BACKING FABRIC

QUILT BATTING,
at least 101 x 118-inches

Instructions

Snowflake Blocks Make 30 blocks

Cutting

From each of the 30 DARK PRINTS:

- Cut 1, 4-1/2 x 42-inch strip. From this strip cut:
  1, 4-1/2-inch square
  8, 2-1/2 x 4-1/2-inch rectangles

- Cut 1, 2-1/2 x 42-inch strip. From this strip cut:
  8, 2-1/2-inch squares

From BEIGE PRINT:

- Cut 45, 2-1/2 x 42-inch strips. From these strips cut:
  720, 2-1/2-inch squares

Piecing

For each snowflake block you will need 24 of the 2-1/2-inch Beige squares and one set of Dark Print pieces (one 4-1/2-inch square, eight 2-1/2 x 4-1/2-inch rectangles, and eight 2-1/2-inch squares).

Step 1   Sew 8 of the 2-1/2-inch Beige squares and the 2-1/2-inch Dark Print squares together in pairs, and press. Sew the pairs together to make 4 Four-Patch units, and press. At this point each Four-Patch unit should measure 4-1/2-inches square.

Make 8

Make 4

Step 2   Position a 2-1/2-inch Beige square on the corner of a 2-1/2 x 4-1/2-inch Dark Print rectangle. Draw a diagonal line on the Beige square, and stitch on the line. Trim the seam allowance to 1/4-inch, and press. Repeat this process at the opposite corner of the Dark Print rectangle. Make 8 units. Sew the units together in pairs, and press. At this point each unit should measure 4-1/2-inches square.

Make 8

Make 4

Step 3   Referring to the block diagram, sew a Step 2 unit to both sides of the 4-1/2-inch Dark Print square, and press. Sew a Four-Patch unit to both sides of the remaining Step 2 units, and press. Sew the 3 horizontal rows together to make a block. At this point the block should measure 12-1/2-inches square.

Step 4   Repeat Steps 1 through 3 to make a total of 30 snowflake blocks.

Quilt Center

Note: The side and corner triangles are larger than necessary and will be trimmed before the borders are added.

Cutting

From BEIGE PRINT:

- Cut 3, 19 x 42-inch strips. From these strips cut:
  5, 19-inch squares. Cut the squares diagonally into quarters for a total of 20 side triangles (you'll only use 18 side triangles).
  2, 10-inch squares. Cut the squares in half diagonally for a total of 4 corner triangles.

- Cut 7, 12-1/2 x 42-inch strips.
  From these strips cut:
  20, 12-1/2 -inch alternate blocks

Assembling the Quilt Center

Step 1   Referring to the quilt diagram, lay out the snowflake blocks, Beige alternate blocks, and Beige side triangles. Sew the pieces together in diagonal rows. Press the seam allowances toward the Beige alternate blocks and side triangles.

Step 2   Pin the rows at the block intersections and sew the rows together. Press the seam allowances in one direction.

Step 3   Sew the Beige corner triangles to the quilt center, and press.

Step 4   Trim away the excess fabric from the side and corner triangles, taking care to allow a 1/4-inch seam allowance beyond the corners of each block. Refer to Trimming the Side and Corner Triangles on page 136.

Borders

Note: The yardage given allows for the border strips to be cut on the crosswise grain. Diagonally piece the strips as needed, referring to page 136 for Diagonal Piecing Instructions.

Cutting

From GOLD PRINT:

- Cut 10, 2-1/2 x 42-inch inner border strips

From GREEN FLORAL:

- Cut 11, 4-1/2 x 42-inch outer border strips

Attaching the Borders

Step 1   To attach the 2-1/2-inch wide Gold inner border strips, refer to page 135 for Border Instructions.

Step 2   To attach the 4-1/2-inch wide Green Floral outer border strips, refer to page 135 for Border Instructions.

Putting It All Together

Cut the 8-5/8 yard length of backing fabric into thirds crosswise to form 3, 2-7/8 yard lengths. Refer to Finishing the Quilt on page 135 for complete instructions.

Binding
Cutting
From GREEN FLORAL:
* Cut 11, 2-3/4 x 42-inch strips

Sew the binding to the quilt using a 3/8-inch seam allowance. This measurement will produce a 1/2-inch wide finished double binding. Refer to page 136 for Binding and Diagonal Piecing Instructions.

Patchwork Snowflake Quilt

a decorator's touch
Ruffled Pillows

Decorator's delight in adding finishing touches to almost everything in the room. Here, the Patchwork Snowflake Quilt is enhanced with accent pillows for the bed in a variety of coordinating prints that feature easy-to-make, extra-wide ruffles for true decorator flair.

Instructions

Fabrics & Supplies

Finished Size:
20 x 26-inch pillow without ruffle

Yardage is based on 42-inch wide fabric

1-3/4 yards
LARGE BROWN FLORAL FLANNEL for
pillow front and back

3/4 yard GOLD PRINT FLANNEL
for mock inner ruffle

1 yard GREEN PRINT FLANNEL
for mock outer ruffle

20 x 26-inch BED PILLOW

Flannel Pillow Sham

Cutting

From LARGE BROWN FLORAL FLANNEL:
- Cut 1, 21 x 27-inch rectangle for pillow front
- Cut 2, 21 x 36-inch rectangles for pillow back

From GOLD PRINT:
- Cut 5, 4-3/4 x 42-inch strips for inner ruffle

From GREEN PRINT:
- Cut 5, 6-3/4 x 42-inch strips for outer ruffle

Attaching the Ruffle

Step 1   Diagonally piece the 4-3/4-inch wide Gold Print strips together. Diagonally piece the 6-3/4-inch wide Green Print strips together, referring to page 136 for Diagonal Piecing Instructions.

Step 2   Aligning long edges, sew the Gold and Green strips together, and press. With right sides facing, sew the short raw edges together with a diagonal seam to make a continuous ruffle strip. Trim the seam allowance to 1/4-inch, and press.

Step 3   Fold the strip in half lengthwise, wrong sides together, and press. Divide the ruffle strip into 4 equal segments, and mark the quarter points with safety pins.

Step 4   To gather the ruffle, position a heavyweight thread (or 2 strands of regular weight sewing thread) 1/4-inch in from the raw edges of the folded ruffle strip.

Note: You will need a length of heavyweight thread 184-inches long. Secure one end of the thread by stitching across it. Zigzag-stitch over the thread all the way around the ruffle, taking care not to sew through it.

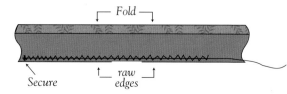

Step 5   Divide the edges of the 21 x 27-inch Large Brown Floral rectangle into 4 equal segments and mark the quarter points with safety pins. With right sides together, pin the ruffle to the pillow front, matching the quarter points of the ruffle to the quarter points of the pillow front. Pull up the gathering stitches until the ruffle fits the pillow front, taking care to allow fullness in the ruffle at each corner. Sew the ruffle to the pillow front, using a 1/4-inch seam allowance.

Assembling the Pillow Back

Step 1   With wrong sides together, fold the 2, 21 x 36-inch Large Brown Floral Flannel rectangles in half to form 2, 17-1/2 x 21-inch double-thick pillow back pieces. Overlap the 2 folded edges by about 5-inches so the pillow back measures 21 x 27-inches, and pin. Stitch around the entire piece to create a single pillow back, using a scant 1/4-inch seam alowance.

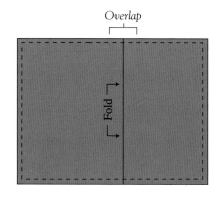

Step 2   With right sides together, layer the pillow back and the pillow front, and pin. The ruffle will be turned toward the center of the pillow at this time. Stitch around the outside edges using a 1/2-inch seam allowance.

Step 3   Trim the pillow back and corner seam allowances if needed. Turn the pillow right side out and fluff up the ruffle. Insert the pillow form through the back opening.

Instructions

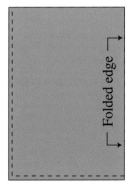

Fabrics & Supplies

Yardage is based on 42-inch wide fabric

1-2/3 yards TAN FLORAL
for pillow front, back, and ruffle

Standard BED PILLOW FORM

Linen Pillowcase

Cutting

Measure the distance around the middle of your pillow form and add 1-inch to the measurement to allow for a 1/2-inch seam allowance. Measure the length of your pillow form and add 1-inch to the measurement to allow for a 1/2-inch seam allowance at each end of the pillowcase.

From TAN FLORAL:

- Cut 1 rectangle according to the measurement determined above for pillowcase

- Cut 2, 13 x 42-inch strips for ruffle

Assembly

Step 1   With right sides together, sew the bottom and side edge of the Tan Floral rectangle to make the pillowcase. Turn the pillowcase right side out.

Folded edge

Attaching the Ruffle

Step 1   Piece the 13-inch wide Tan Floral strips together to make a continuous ruffle strip.

Step 2   Fold the strip in half lengthwise, wrong sides together, and press.

Step 3   To gather the ruffle, position a heavyweight thread (or 2 strands of regular weight sewing thread) 1/4-inch in from the raw edges of the folded ruffle strip (refer to Flannel Pillow Sham gathering diagram on page 50).

Note: You will need a length of heavyweight thread 84-inches long. Secure one end of the thread by stitching across it. Zigzag-stitch over the thread all the way around the ruffle, taking care not to sew through it.

Step 4   With raw edges even and right sides together, position the ruffle on the pillowcase. Distribute the ruffle fullness evenly while pulling up the gathering thread until the ruffle fits the edge of the pillowcase, and pin. Sew the ruffle in place using a 1/2-inch seam allowance. Zigzag-stitch over the raw edges to prevent fraying.

autumn accents
Leaf-stenciled Walls

These falling leaves never need raking! For a bedroom that transcends the seasons,
the colors of the Patchwork Snowflake Quilt blend with the golds and greens of the stencil
paints used for the autumn leaves. The full-size stencils are provided, opposite. Turn the
page for a variety of ways to combine the leaves in attractive groupings.

Instructions

Supplies

All supplies are available from hobby or craft stores.

LATEX WALL PAINT

TEMPLATE PLASTIC
(if you are cutting your own stencils)or
VARIETY OF PURCHASED STENCILS

STENCIL PAINTS AND BRUSHES

Stenciling

Step 1   Paint walls a neutral color. Rag or sponge a slightly lighter color for added interest.

Step 2   Using the stencil paints, stencil the shapes on the wall. Work with a very small amount of paint on the stencil brush, pounding the brush lightly to apply the paint. Apply paint at the edges of the cut-out, working toward the center. The variation of color between the lighter and darker areas enhances the hand-painted effect.

Leaf Templates

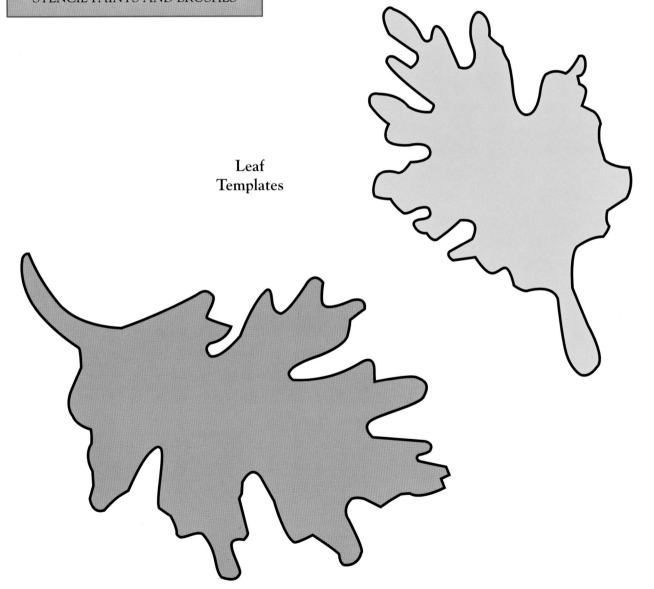

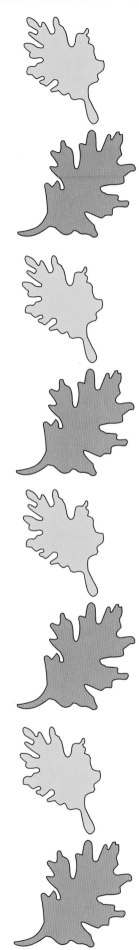

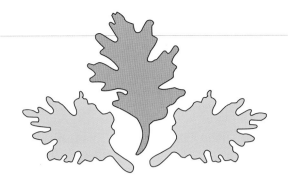

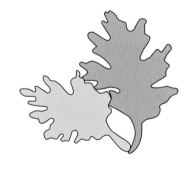

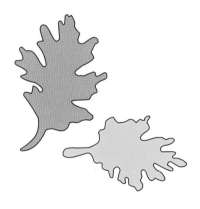

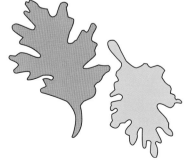

a beginner's dream
Big Block Quilt

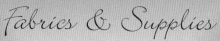

The perfect project for beginners or for power quilters who want to finish it fast!

Fabrics & Supplies

Finished Size: 72 x 84-inches

Yardage is based on 42-inch wide fabric

42, 15-inch ASSORTED FLANNEL squares

1-7/8 yards RED PRINT for binding

5 yards BACKING FABRIC

QUILT BATTING, at least 76 x 88-inches

Instructions

Blocks

Cutting

From ASSORTED FLANNEL:

• Cut 42, 12-1/2-inch squares

Piecing

Step 1   Referring to the quilt diagram, sew the 12-1/2-inch Assorted Flannel blocks together in 7 rows of 6 blocks each. Press the seam allowances in alternating directions by rows so the seams will fit snugly together with less bulk.

Step 2   Pin the rows together at the block intersections, and sew the rows together. Press the seam allowances in one direction.

Putting It All Together

Cut the 5 yard length of backing fabric in half crosswise to make 2, 2-1/2 yard lengths. Refer to Finishing the Quilt on page 135 for complete instructions.

Binding

Cutting

From RED PRINT:

• Cut 9, 6-1/2 x 42-inch strips

Sew the binding to the quilt using a scant 1-inch seam allowance. This measurement will produce a 1-inch wide finished double binding. Refer to page 136 for Binding and Diagonal Piecing Instructions.

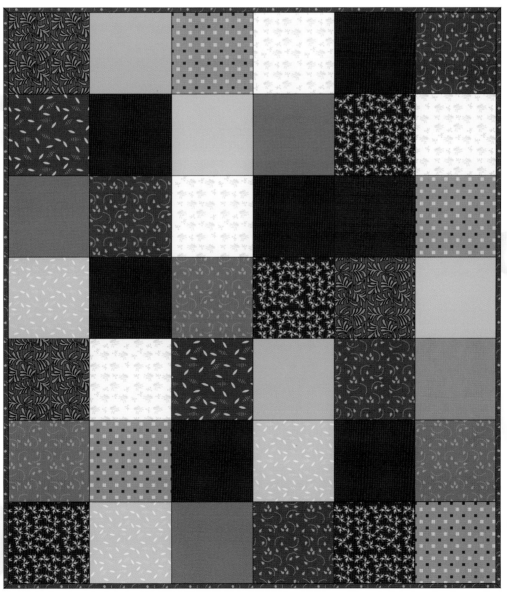

Big Block Quilt

fun, freezer paper flowers
Tulip Garden Quilt

Using freezer paper templates for the flowers and leaves makes it easy to hand-appliqué them in the center of each tulip block.

Fabrics & Supplies

Finished Size: 37-3/4 x 49-inches

Yardage is based on 42-inch wide fabric

5/8 yard MUSLIN for appliqué foundation

1-1/2 yards BEIGE FLORAL
for alternate blocks, side and
corner triangles, and outer border

1/4 yard GREEN PRINT for inner border

1/3 yard SOLID GREEN
for stem and leaf appliqués

3-inch squares of 36
ASSORTED PRINTS for flower appliqués

1/2 yard GREEN PRINT for binding

1-1/2 yards BACKING FABRIC

QUILT BATTING, at least 42 x 53-inches

1/2 yard FREEZER PAPER for appliqué

Instructions

Appliqué the Tulip Blocks

Make 6 blocks

Note: Make a template of the entire flower shape to use as a Placement Guide for the individual flower shapes. To do so, photocopy the shape on page 61, glue the paper to a manila folder to stabilize it, and cut out the shape. Use the outer portion for the template and discard the inner portion.

Cutting

From MUSLIN:

- Cut 2, 8-3/4 x 42-inch strips. From these strips cut: 6, 8-3/4-inch appliqué foundation squares

From SOLID GREEN:

- Cut 6, 1-3/8 x 6-inch bias strips

- Cut 6, 1-3/8 x 4-inch bias strips

Appliqué the Stems

Step 1   Fold a 1-3/8 x 6-inch Solid Green bias strip in half lengthwise with wrong sides together, and press. To keep the raw edges aligned, stitch 1/4-inch away from the edges. Fold the strip in half again so the raw edges are hidden by the first folded edge, and press. Position the Placement Guide on an 8-3/4-inch Muslin square, aligning bottom edges. Simply lay the stem inside this shape for placement. Pin the stem in place.

Step 2   In the same manner, prepare a 1-3/8 x 4-inch Solid Green bias strip. Pin the stem in place on the Muslin square, tucking one end under the 6-inch long stem. Hand-stitch the stems in place. Make 6 blocks.

Flower and Leaf Appliqué
(Freezer Paper Technique)

Note: With this method of hand appliqué, the freezer paper forms a base around which each flower and leaf is shaped.

Step 1   Lay a piece of freezer paper, paper side up, over a leaf shape, and use a pencil to trace this shape 12 times. Cut out the leaves on the traced lines.

Step 2   With a dry iron on the wool setting, press the coated side of each freezer paper leaf onto the wrong side of the Solid Green leaf fabric. Allow at least 1/2-inch between each shape for seam allowances.

Step 3   Cut out each leaf a scant 1/4-inch beyond the edge of the freezer paper pattern and finger-press the seam allowance over the edge of the freezer paper.

Step 4   Position 2 leaves on the Muslin square using the Placement Guide. Appliqué the leaves with matching thread. When there is about 3/4-inch left to appliqué on each leaf, slide your needle into this opening and loosen the freezer paper. Gently remove it, and finish stitching each leaf in place. Repeat on the remaining 5 Muslin squares.

Step 5   In the same manner, prepare the flower centers, trace 12 times. Appliqué the flower centers on the Muslin squares.

Step 6   In the same manner, prepare the flower petals, tracing 12 and 12 reversed. Appliqué the petals on the Muslin squares.

Quilt Center

Note: The side and corner triangles are larger than necessary and will be trimmed before the borders are added.

Cutting

From BEIGE FLORAL:

- Cut 1, 14 x 42-inch strip. From this strip cut: 2, 14-inch squares. Cut the squares diagonally into quarters, forming 8 triangles. You will be using only 6 for side triangles.

- Cut 1, 9 x 42-inch strip. From this strip cut: 2, 9-inch squares. Cut the squares in half diagonally for a total of 4 corner triangles. 2, 8-3/4-inch squares for the alternate blocks

Assembling the Quilt Center

Step 1   Referring to the quilt diagram, sew together the 6 appliquéd blocks, 2 alternate blocks, and 6 side triangles in diagonal rows. Press the seam allowances in alternating directions by rows so the seams will fit snugly together with less bulk.

Step 2   Pin the rows at the block intersections, and sew the rows together. Press the seam allowances in one direction.

Step 3   Sew the 4 corner triangles to the quilt center, and press.

Step 4   Trim away the excess fabric from the side and corner triangles, taking care to allow a 1/4-inch seam allowance beyond the corners of each block. Refer to Trimming the Side and Corner Triangles on page 136 for complete instructions.

Borders

Note: *The yardage given allows for the border strips to be cut on the crosswise grain. Diagonally piece the strips as needed, referring to page 136 for Diagonal Piecing Instructions.*

Cutting

From GREEN PRINT:

- Cut 4, 1-1/2 x 42-inch inner border strips

From BEIGE FLORAL:

- Cut 4, 6-1/2 x 42-inch outer border strips

Attaching the Borders

Step 1 To attach the 1-1/2-inch wide Green inner border strips, refer to page 135 for Border Instructions.

Step 2 To attach the 6-1/2-inch wide Beige Floral outer border strips, refer to page 135 for Border Instructions.

Putting It All Together

Trim the backing and batting so they are 4-inches larger than the quilt top. Refer to Finishing the Quilt on page 136 for complete instructions.

Binding

Cutting

From GREEN PRINT:

- Cut 5, 2-3/4 x 42-inch strips

Sew the binding to the quilt using a 3/8-inch seam allowance. This measurement will produce a 1/2-inch wide finished double binding. Refer to page 136 for Binding and Diagonal Piecing Instructions.

Tulip Garden Quilt

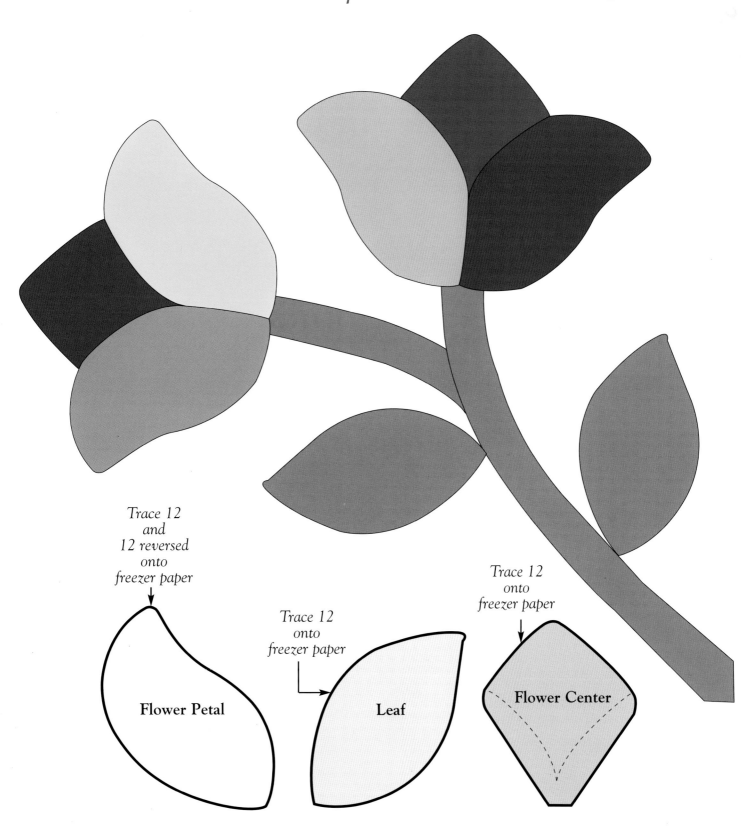

Trace 12
and
12 reversed
onto
freezer paper

Flower Petal

Trace 12
onto
freezer paper

Leaf

Trace 12
onto
freezer paper

Flower Center

cottage
Gardens

or Lynette, the secret to creating country-cottage style comfort is surrounding the cottage with the glories of a cottage garden.

The idea of a cottage garden appeals to her practical nature as well. There is no need for a big budget and no need to be a gardening expert. The cottage garden works well in small spaces just as it did in the tiny parcels of land surrounding the English cottages from which it evolved. In fact, in helping Kerry and Trevor design and plan the gardens in their small suburban yard, Lynette took full advantage of window boxes and container gardening.

In a true cottage garden, random plantings of tall plants such as hollyhocks and sunflowers can easily be inter-planted with everything from herbs to vegetables. This dense planting saves work because it keeps out weeds and tall plants can lean on each other for support.

Lynette's busy lifestyle as a business-owner calls for a no-nonsense approach to gardening. Plants and flowers must be hardy enough to take care of themselves, and Lynette is fond of saying, "Work with me." If the plants don't cooperate, out they go!

To create the dried floral arrangements scattered about Kerry and Trevor's home, Lynette first grew many of the plants and flowers in her own cutting garden. She is shown, opposite, with a sampling of the abundance of plantings harvested from her garden. Many of the flowering plants were divided and transplanted into Kerry and Trevor's newly-created garden last spring.

On the following pages, you'll find Lynette's tips and techniques for an easy-to-manage cottage garden. Before you know it, you'll be creating your own little piece of heaven on earth!

Relax and enjoy. For busy career couples like Kerry and Trevor, Lynette recommends lots of low maintenance plantings, preferably in easy-care window boxes or clay pots and containers.

The antique child's cupboard shown below, makes a perfect storage unit for oversized gardening books and small collectible flower pots.

From homely to homey. As with many of the older homes in Minneapolis, parking is in the back and most home-owners park the car and walk past the garage to enter by the back door.

The only distinguising feature of Kerry and Trevor's garage was a plain off-center window and lots of bare ground and gravel.

Lynette suggested simply screening the garage window, left, with a cost-effective 8-foot fence panel and using the balance of the wall for a potting table.

Create instant curb appeal. After taking on a mortage, most new homeowners have little left over to spend on luxuries like extensive landscaping. However, a fresh coat of paint and a few strategic plantings can transform a home's exterior.

Here, window boxes filled with blooms along with pots of plants on the steps and a variety of plants lining the sidewalk, soften the view and offer a warm welcome reminiscent of an English cottage.

The child's Adirondack chair, below, showcases a poem that Kerry penned at the age of seven. Lynette saved the original and recently had it stitched in embroidery and fabric-matted in a frame as a keepsake for Kerry. The poem is a fitting tribute to Kerry's love for nature as she establishes her own cottage garden.

Spring
The leaves are
uncurling.
My seedlings are
up. The sunlight
is warmer. We've
got a new pup.
The robins are
building. I've painted
my bike. And we
can go barefoot
whenever we like.

Kerry
Age 7

Cover a lot of ground. Plants such as Shasta daisies and cone flowers are inexpensive, hardy, and even handy for visiting butterflies!

Because they bloom in abundance all summer, Lynette plants plenty of them in beds and borders throughout the garden for a steady supply of stems for cutting. She finds them particularly useful as filler for bucketfuls of bouquets.

Combine annuals and perennials. Flowering plants come in all shapes and sizes. In a window box, Lynette suggests annuals such as brightly-colored impatiens and gently trailing licorice leaf.

Choose Rudbikea (right) for height and enduring color in the garden and choose Annabelle Hydrangea (lower right) for large blooms from summer through autumn. Both perennials are maintenance-free and hardy enough to survive even Minnesota's winters.

Lynette is particularly fond of hydrangeas because they serve the garden from summer to early autumn. She picks the blooms in late summer when they have turned from white to green and feel dry to the touch like parchment paper. If picked at just the right time, the dry hydrangea blossoms can be used in dried arrangements well into the winter.

Blossoms that are allowed to remain on the plant into late fall turn a golden bronze color and make spectacular autumn bouquets.

Divide and conquer. Save time and energy by starting tiny plants such as individual begonias in big pots. Fill the empty space with smaller clay pots like the ones shown at left. They hold later-blooming plants such as marigolds and can be easily removed as the begonia grows to full size.

The smooth river rocks shown below serve as inconspicuous plant markers and can be placed directly under the plant for easy reference.

Use a permanent black marker for printing names of plants directly onto the smoothest surface of the rocks. At the end of the season the river rocks can be collected and stored in a wire basket to be used again the following spring.

Discover hardworking decorations.
Antique ironwork shown above is used to decorate the garden as well as serve as staking for taller plants. An elevated iron plant stand filled with brightly-colored blooms lends added height and depth to the cottage garden.

The old enamel sauce pan brings back memories of yesteryear, but is as hardworking today as it was then. Here, it is used for keeping garden twine handy when tying up and staking plants. The pan keeps the twine from tangling and rolling out of sight and the handle makes it easy to grab and go!

low maintenance
Living Wreath

Lynette was first treated to a living wreath by her neighbor's 15-year-old daughter, Mary. The wreath is shown in full, above, and in it's earliest stage on the opposite page. Planted with chicks and hens and a variety of sedum nestled in sphagnum moss, the wreath filled in throughout the summer and was also used as a candle ring around a glass chimney resting on a large terra cotta saucer on the patio table.

Supplies

All supplies are available from hobby, craft or garden stores.

WIRE WREATH FORM

POTTING SOIL

18 GAUGE WIRE

SPHAGNUM MOSS

ASSORTED SEDUM PLANTS

Living Wreath

Step 1   Lay sphagnum moss under wire frame. Moss should be wide enought to pull up and wrap around wire frame.

Step 2   Fill frame with potting soil.

Step 3   Bring moss up and around wire frame holding in soil.

Step 4   Wrap wire around frame holding in soil.

Step 5   Water wreath thouroughly.

Step 6   Poke a small hole in moss and soil and insert plants carefully.

Step 7   Press soil firmly around roots to hold plants in place.

Most sedum are succulent or semi-succulent plant types, so water only as needed, and enjoy your living wreath month after month.

great for dried floral displays
Decoupaged Tins

Vintage postcards and old tins team up with dried flowers from the garden for rustic country-cottage style table top displays. The large tin shown above was Kerry's great-grandmother's seed tin. Lynette first made color copies of cards from her collection, and then decoupaged them to the tin in a random fashion.

Instructions

Supplies

RUSTIC OR GALVANIZED TINS

LATEX WALL PAINT (optional)

MODGE PODGE GLUE®

VINTAGE POSTCARDS or
Photocopied Reproductions
from the following pages

Decoupage

Step 1   Leave the tin in it's natural state or paint it
with any color latex paint you like. Let dry for 4 hours.

Step 2   Trim copies of vintage postcards as desired.

Step 3   Cover the tin with Modge Podge Glue®. While the glue is still
wet, position the cut-out shapes on the tin. Work in areas, apply-
ing Modge Podge Glue® as you go. Let dry for 4 hours.

Step 4   To seal the surface of the tin, cover the tin once again with Modge
Podge Glue®. Let dry for 4 hours.

Try anything. Most photo-copied reproductions of the vintage postcards will adhere to almost any surface with Modge Podge Glue®. Use reproductions of your own vintage cards, or simply photocopy the cards from Lynette's personal collection featured on the following pages. Examples of containers that work well for decoupage include a watering can and an old sap bucket as shown at left.

The vintage postcards on these two pages are from Lynette's personal collection.
Permission is granted to photocopy for your personal use only.

Greetings on Your
Birthday

May winds blow fair
and skies be blue
And every day bring
joy to you

BIRTHDAY
GREETINGS

A Happy Birthday

The vintage postcards on these two pages are from Lynette's personal collection.
Permission is granted to photocopy for your personal use only.

The vintage postcards on these two pages are from Lynette's personal collection.
Permission is granted to photocopy for your personal use only.

forever in bloom
Potpourri

Flowers from the cottage garden will be forever in bloom when you fill a basket or bowl with potpourri.
Deadheading all blossoms throughout the summer will give an abundance of petals as well as make the plants thrive.
Let the petals dry on newspaper away from humidity and bright sunlight before adding them to the potpourri mix.

Instructions

Supplies

ROSES, any color

BABY'S BREATH

MONEY PLANT

BITTERSWEET

BACHELOR'S BUTTON

FORGET-ME-NOT
(or most any of your favorite flowers)

Drying flowers

Step 1   Pick flowers at their freshest.

Step 2   For bouquets, tie stems of blossoms together and hang upside down to dry away from humidity and bright sunlight.

Step 3   For individual blossoms, spread them out and allow to dry on newspapers. For potpourri, simply drop any deadheaded blooms into the container and allow to dry and add fragrance to the mix.

Although it requires more time and effort, you can use silica gel to dry flowers, especially more complex blooms. Silica gel can be bought at most hobby and craft stores, and some florists. Follow manufacturer's instructions for using the gel (which is actually like a very fine white sand).

Look for variety. Finding an unusual container for an interesting potpourri mix is only limited by your imagination.
Here a wooden bowl fills up quickly with dry leaves and a single hydrangea blossom added for texture.

While working with Kerry and Trevor in planning their cottage garden, Lynette decided to begin
keeping a journal of plans and progress. She also included a plant schematic and
listing of the plants with notations for care after planting. Adding "before and after" photographs and
decorative accents makes this personalized keepsake hardworking but handsome.

Instructions

Supplies

SCRAPBOOK

"Before and After" PICTURES

GARDENING INFORMATION such as Landscape Drawings, Planting Dates and Locations, Care Instructions, Weather, Growth and Bloom Data

PRESSED FLOWERS

DECORATIVE PAPERS/STICKERS

Garden Journal

Step 1   Make this a workbook as well as a scrapbook. Use it as a way to stay in touch with your garden, learning as you go.

Step 2   Begin by making or purchasing a blank scrapbook. Use acid-free decorative papers, stickers, and pressed flowers for accents.

Step 3   Take "before and after" photographs of your garden in progress and use acid-free tape to secure them to the pages.

Step 4   Finish with ribbon ties glued to the insides of the front and back covers, if desired.

fabric framed
Botanical Prints

*Since country-cottage style decorating is inspired by florals, framed botanicals for the wall
are a fine finishing touch. Lynette color-coordinates them to her quilts, pillows, and other soft comforts
by combining small blocks of Thimbleberries® fabrics and fusing them to a mat for each print.*

Instructions

Fabrics & Supplies

MAT BOARD
Cut 1-inch larger than finished size

COTTON PRINT
to coordinate with Botanical Print

PAPER-BACKED FUSIBLE WEB

Patchwork-like Mat Board

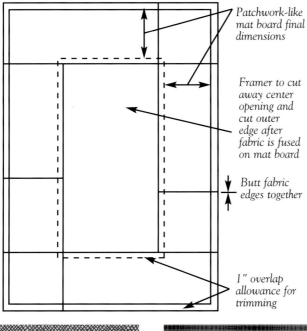

Patchwork-like
mat board final
dimensions

Framer to cut
away center
opening and
cut outer
edge after
fabric is fused
on mat board

Butt fabric
edges together

1" overlap
allowance for
trimming

Mat Board Assembly

Step 1   Cut the cotton print 2-inches larger than the mat board.

Step 2   Cut the fusible web 1-inch larger than the mat board.

Step 3   Following the manufacturer's instructions, apply the fusible web to the wrong side of the cotton print. Let the fabric cool. Peel away the paper backing from the fusible web. Fuse the fabric to the mat board.

Step 4   Have a professional framing shop cut your fabric-covered mat board and frame your print.

Optional: To achieve a patchwork-like mat board, apply fusible web to various size pieces of coordinating fabrics.

- Referring to the diagram at left, cut the fused fabrics so that they extend 1-inch beyond the outer edge of the mat board and 1-inch beyond the desired finished inner edge of the mat board. It is very important that the fabric edges are clean and straight because the fused fabrics will butt up against each other. Do not overlap the edges.

- Refer to the steps above to complete the mat board.

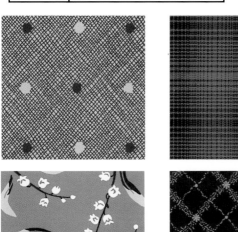

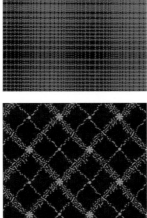

Garden Party

Start a new tradition. For an inviting, old-fashioned garden party, a vintage Grandmother's Flower Garden quilt tops off a sturdy wooden ironing board stained and varnished to be used as a side table on the patio. On a warm summer day, Lynette gathered a group of friends who brought starter plants to pass along to Kerry for her new garden.

Garden Party
Invitations

Presentation is part of the gift. Hand-delivered invitations to the garden party consisted of a flower pot painted antique white and trimmed with vintage buttons glued to the rim. The pot held garden gloves, plant markers, and a package of flower seeds with the invitation glued to the back. Each invited guest was encouraged to fill the painted pot with a favorite plant from her garden and bring it to the party to share for Kerry's new garden.

Starter Plants

Before the garden party, Lynette spruced up an old step ladder with a fresh coat of paint and put it to work again—this time displaying the potted plants as guests arrive for the afternoon. (The quickly refurbished ladder serves as a useful plant stand indoors or outdoors.)

Lynette is shown below helping guests Sherry and Kathy as they find parking places for the plants brought from home. Plant markers which were labeled with the guest's name when delivered as part of the invitation do double-duty as a gift tag identifying the giver as well as the name of the plant that's been given.

A Garden Party

Please join us for a day in the sun!

Sowing Time: Saturday, May 5, 11:00 am
Preparation: Bring your favorite seeds or bedding plants and pot for planting.
Where to Plant: 2724 Webster Avenue South St. Louis Park
Fertilization: Lunch will be served at noon with plant... below.

Instructions

Supplies

TERRA COTTA FLOWER POTS
4 to 5-inches in Diameter

CREAM ACRYLIC PAINT or SPRAY PAINT

Assorted CREAM/WHITE BUTTONS

GARDEN GLOVES

FLOWER SEED PACKETS

PURCHASED or
HANDMADE PARTY INVITATIONS

WOOD PLANT MARKERS

MARKING PEN

SANDPAPER

HOT GLUE GUN

Assembly

Step 1   Paint terra cotta flower pots, with cream-colored paint.

Step 2   Lightly sand rim of pot to expose a little of the terra cotta color.

Step 3   Hot glue buttons to the top band of the pot.

Step 4   Glue party invitation to the back of the seed packet.

Step 5   Fill the pot with gloves, seed packet/invitation, and plant marker with guest's name.

Step 6   Hand deliver the invitation.

A Garden Party

Please join us for a day in the sun!

Sowing Time: Date

Preparation: Bring your favorite seeds or bedding plants and a pot for planting

Where to Plant: Address

Fertilization: Lunch will be served at noon

As Virginia and other guests continue to arrive bearing gifts of plants, Lynette serves iced tea
in old-fashioned glasses from a tabletop filled with vintage dishes, tins, ceramic pots,
and luncheon cloth and napkins from the 1930s. Here, Sue admires the centerpiece bouquet arranged in
an unusual round tin complete with a cottage garden and the proverbial white picket fence.

Trellis Planters

In the photo above, Kathy examines a circa 1930 Dresden Plate quilt in bright garden colors shown solo on a trellis planter.

All good things must come to an end, and departing guests are treated to bottles of herb vinegars and jars of rich, moisterizing hand balm made by a local gardener.

Display it differently. Much of the fun of a party is seeing everyone and everything dressed for the occasion. Ardelle, in the summer straw hat, and Sherry visit beside a vintage flower cart filled with plants and floral bouquets. In the background, Renae and Lisa discover trellis planters nestled in the flower garden which are used for displaying several quilts from Lynette's extensive collection of antique quilts.

In the kitchen, Swanky Swig glasses from the 1930s era, and cozy curtains stitched up from old tablecloths lend an air of cottage comfort to the luncheon food preparation.

Greek Pasta Salad

Dressing:

2/3 cup olive oil

3 T. white vinegar

1/4 cup chopped fresh basil

2 T. chopped green onions

2 T. grated Parmesan cheese

1/2 tsp. salt

1/4 tsp. pepper

1/4 tsp. oregano leaves

Salad:

8 oz. uncooked tri-colored spiral macaroni

1 sm. green bell pepper, cut into 1/4" strips

1 sm. red bell pepper, cut into 1/4" strips

1 med. tomato, cut into wedges
   or cherry tomatoes, cut in half

1/2 cup pitted and sliced Greek olives

8 oz. sliced pepperoni

6 oz. feta cheese, crumbled

Combine all dressing ingredients in blender, blend until smooth. Cook macaroni until tender. Drain; rinse with cold water. Combine all salad ingredients. Pour dressing over salad; toss gently. Refrigerate 1 hour to blend flavors.

Makes 10 servings.

Note: Lynette painted terra cotta plant saucers and lined them with clear plastic plant trays prior to using them as salad bowls. Be sure that food for consumption does not come in direct contact with unglazed or unprotected painted surfaces.

Swiss Poppy Seed Bread

1 loaf French bread

1 cup butter, melted

1/2 cup chopped onion

1/4 cup poppy seeds

1 lb. Swiss cheese, sliced

Cut loaf of French bread into 10 slices, 3/4-way through. Insert slices of Swiss cheese between each of the bread slices. Sauté onion in butter until onion is translucent, not brown. Add poppy seeds to butter. Spoon butter/onion/poppy seed mixture between the slices of bread and cheese.

Wrap in foil. Bake at 300 degrees until the cheese melts and bread is hot throughout (approximately 20 minutes).

Makes 10 servings.

cottage Celebrations

ountry-cottage style decorating offers you the opportunity to celebrate your independence from rigid, traditional decorating rules, since almost anything goes—as long it makes you feel comfortable and relaxed.

The same goes for celebrating in country-cottage style. If your space is small, move everything to the great outdoors. If your space is large, bring everyone together in a cozy corner of the family room for game day food and festivities as you celebrate your team's victory.

Regardless of the size of your room or your crowd, the emphasis is on comfort and making harmony the heart of the home. On the pages that follow, Lynette takes you through the seasons with ideas and inspirations for everything from a parade day picnic to a pumpkin carving party—old-fashioned fun celebrated in casual country-cottage style. From the invitations to the decorations and food to the party favors, you'll find everything you need to make entertaining so easy you'll feel like a guest in your own home!

Shower your guests with gifts. The romance of country-cottage style is in full bloom when it comes to hosting a bridal shower. Prior to her wedding, Lynette's daughter Kerry was the recipient of several bridal showers. Now as her friends anticipate marriage, she can reciprocate by helping them celebrate in a casual, but special way. A gift box favor for each guest holds a photo frame for a photo-memory of the party to be sent to guests as a reminder of the festivities.

You Are Invited to a Bridal Shower!

Date
Saturday, June 16

Time

Bridal Shower
Invitations

More uses for cottage garden flowers. Even a simple invitation to a bridal shower becomes a keepsake with the addition of dried flowers from the garden. For the invitation shown below, Lynette collected mallow blossoms, pressed them between the pages of a phone book, and glued them to the front of a folder created to hold the invitation.

If you are really "pressed for time," floral stickers can just as easily be substituted for the real thing.

Gift Boxes

To make the gift boxes, Lynette and Kerry started with lidded paper maché boxes from the craft store. They painted each box cream and added a delicate border of stenciled leaves.

After a tissue-wrapped photo frame was nestled into each box, the lid was added and both box and lid tied together with an elegant sheer gold ribbon topped off with a nosegay of dried blossoms tucked into the bow.

You Are Invited
to a
Bridal Shower!

Date
Saturday, June 16

Time

Sugar Cookies

2 cups butter, softened

2 cups sugar

1 egg

1 tsp. vanilla

1/4 tsp. salt

1 tsp. baking powder

4-1/4 cups flour

Cream butter, sugar, egg and vanilla until fluffy. Combine dry ingredients; stir into creamed mixture just until blended. Divide and shape dough into four, 2" round logs. Refrigerate, covered, at least 2 hours or overnight.

Preheat oven to 375 degrees. Slice roll into 1/4" slices and bake until edges are golden brown (approximately 8 minutes). Remove to wire rack to cool.

Makes 8–9 dozen.

Vanilla Creme Sauce

1 cup heavy whipping cream

1 cup sour cream

4 T. sugar

2 tsp. vanilla

Whisk to blend ingredients. Cover and refrigerate for several hours.

Tops 10–12 desserts.

Salted Nut Bars

1, 9" x 13" white cake

1, 8 oz. can honey roasted peanuts, chopped

Powdered Sugar Almond Frosting (from recipe below)

Cut cake into 18 pieces. Frost all sides with frosting. Place chopped nuts on waxed paper and roll frosted cake pieces in nuts, coating all sides.

Allow frosting to dry slightly before serving.

Makes 18.

Powdered Sugar Almond Frosting

2 cups powdered sugar

1/3 cup milk

1 tsp. almond extract

Mix until smooth. Use to frost salted nut bars or your favorite cakes and cookies.

Table Settings

Easy but elegant. Sometimes setting a festive table requires only the extra touch of a rolled linen napkin, ribbon-tied and accented with a tiny dried rosebud. (Note: working with a small piece of the same kind of ribbon used for the party favor gift box will give a coordinated look to each place setting.)

fun, food, and family
Parade Day Picnic

Spark culinary fireworks with summertime favorites. Make it your best Fourth of July ever with flags, food, and fun before the evening fireworks. Gather friends and family following the community celebration for a sumptuous buffet of the season's bounty. Garden-fresh vegetables are used as table decor, and an old childhood wagon holding plants and flowers adds to the spirit of fun. The picnic table, a hand-me-down from Kerry's grandmother, has been white-washed and stenciled with stars and rays, says it all—Celebrate!

Invitations

Get lots of bang for your buck. Symbols of holiday tradition and free-spirited fun—hand-delivered firecracker invitations are attention-getting and surprisingly inexpensive when you make them yourself. Start with a 12-inch mailing tube painted red and sprinkled with gold star stickers. Size your printed invitation to fit, roll it up and slide it inside the mailing tube. For the fuse, cut a small slit-in the cap and insert a 4-inch piece of twisted red/white rope.

Make an extra dozen mailing-tube firecrackers and arrange them in a blue enamel pail on the day of the picnic as a complement to the patriotic theme of red, white, and blue.

Vintage Blue

Above. the vintage blue enameled pail fits nicely into the same-style pan with room to spare. Both are filled with shaved ice to hold chilled beverages.

Below, a vintage blue kettle is large enough to hold a mixture of garden flowers and herbs including zinnias, Bells of Ireland, snapdragons, perennial grasses and statice for an explosion of parade day color.

Parade Day Table

Hurray for the red, white, and blue. A quilted runner and flag napkins set the scene for the patriotic fun and food to come. These projects work up quickly, especially the napkins featuring a small parade flag in the center block. The star and rays templates on page 106 serve a dual purpose—as a star stencil for the table top and as a quilting pattern for the border of the table runner.

Instructions

Fabrics & Supplies

Finished Size: 16-inches square

Makes 4 napkins

Yardage is based on 42-inch wide fabric

7/8 yard GOLD PRINT for border

1 yard BLUE PRINT for napkin back

4, 8-1/2" x 11-1/2" FLAGS

Note: Alter the fabric measurements if using a different size flag.

Flag Napkins

Cutting

From GOLD PRINT:
- Cut 3, 4-1/2 x 42-inch border strips
- Cut 4, 3 x 42-inch border strips

From BLUE PRINT:
- Cut 2, 16-1/2 x 42-inch strips.
  From these strips cut: 4, 16-1/2-inch squares

Piecing

Step 1   Sew 4-1/2-inch wide Gold borders to the top and bottom of the flag, and press. Trim the ends even with the flag.

Step 2   Sew 3-inch wide Gold borders to the sides of the flag, and press. Trim the ends even with the flag. Repeat for a total of 4 napkin fronts.

Make 4

Step 3   With right sides together, layer a 16-1/2-inch pieced napkin front and a 16-1/2-inch Blue square napkin back. Sew 1/4-inch from the cut edges, leaving 3-inches open on one side for turning.

Step 4   Clip the corners, turn the napkin right side out and press, taking care to see that the corners are sharp and even. Hand-stitch the opening closed.

Step 5   Stitch diagonally from corner to corner to stabilize the napkin.

Step 6   Repeat Steps 3 through 5 to make a total of 4 napkins.

Make 4

Supplies

All supplies are available from hobby or craft stores.

LATEX WALL PAINT

TEMPLATE PLASTIC
(if you are cutting your own stencils)or
VARIETY OF PURCHASED STENCILS

STENCIL PAINTS AND BRUSHES

The Star Stencil Template on the following page can be used for the picnic table top or as a quilting pattern for the table runner.

Star-stenciled Tabletop

Step 1   Paint table a neutral color. Rag or sponge a slightly lighter color for added interest.

Step 2   Using the stencil paints, stencil star shapes on the table. Work with a small amount of paint on the stencil brush, pounding the brush lightly to apply the paint at the edges of the cut-out, working toward the center. The variation of color between the lighter and darker areas enhances the hand-painted effect.

Star Stencil Template

Cut out on solid lines for use as a stencil.
Trace dashed lines for use as a quilting pattern.

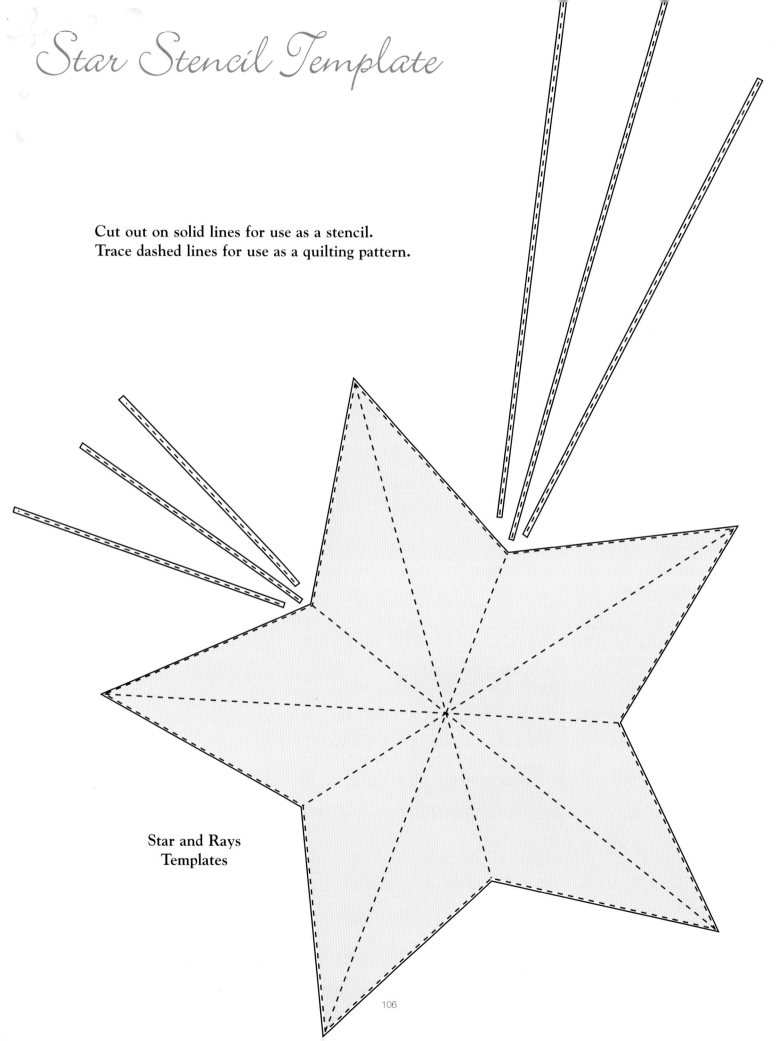

**Star and Rays
Templates**

Step 2 Sew Step 1 star point units to the top and bottom of a 4-1/2-inch Gold square. Press the seam allowances toward the Gold square. Sew 2-1/2-inch Blue Grid squares to the ends of the remaining star point units. Press the seam allowances toward the Blue Grid squares. Sew the units to the sides of the star unit, and press.

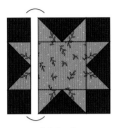

Make 3

Step 3 Aligning long edges, sew together the 2-1/2 x 42-inch Red strips and 1-1/2 x 42-inch Beige strips. Press the seam allowances toward the Red strips. Cut the strip set into segments.

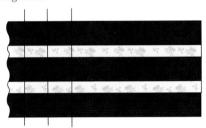

Crosscut 12,
2-1/2-inch wide segments

Step 4 Sew Step 3 units to the top and bottom of the star units, and press. Add 2-1/2-inch Gold squares to the ends of the remaining Step 3 units, and press. Sew the units to the sides of the star units to complete each star block, and press.

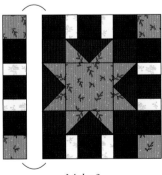

Make 3

Fabrics & Supplies

Finished Size: 22 x 50-inches

Yardage is based on 42-inch wide fabric

3/8 yard GOLD PRINT for stars and blocks

1/3 yard BLUE GRID for blocks

1/3 yard RED PRINT for blocks

1/8 yard BEIGE PRINT for blocks

3/4 yard BLUE PRINT for lattice and border

1/2 yard RED PRINT for binding

1-1/2 yards BACKING FABRIC

QUILT BATTING, at least 26 x 54-inches

Picnic Table Runner

Blocks Make 3 blocks

Cutting

From GOLD PRINT:
- Cut 1, 4-1/2 x 42-inch strip. From this strip cut: 3, 4-1/2-inch squares
- Cut 3, 2-1/2 x 42-inch strips. From these strips cut: 36, 2-1/2-inch squares

From BLUE GRID:
- Cut 1, 2-1/2 x 42-inch strip. From this strip cut: 12, 2-1/2-inch squares
- Cut 2, 2-1/2 x 42-inch strips. From these strips cut: 12, 2-1/2 x 4-1/2-inch rectangles

From RED PRINT:
- Cut 3, 2-1/2 x 42-inch strips

From BEIGE PRINT:
- Cut 2, 1-1/2 x 42-inch strips

Piecing

Step 1 Position a 2-1/2-inch Gold square on the corner of a 2-1/2 x 4-1/2-inch Blue Grid rectangle. Draw a diagonal line on the Gold square, and stitch on the line. Trim the seam allowance to 1/4-inch, and press. Repeat this process at the opposite corner of the Blue Grid rectangle.

Make 12 star points

Quilt Center and Border

Note: The yardage given allows for the border strips to be cut on the crosswise grain. Diagonally piece the strips as needed, referring to page 136 for Diagonal Piecing Instructions.

Cutting

From BLUE PRINT:

- Cut 4, 5-1/2 x 42-inch border strips

- Cut 1, 2-1/2 x 42-inch strip. From this strip cut:
  2, 2-1/2 x 12-1/2-inch lattice strips

Assembly

Step 1   Sew together the 3 pieced blocks and the 2-1/2 x 12-1/2-inch Blue lattice strips, and press.

Step 2   To attach the 5-1/2-inch wide Blue Print border strips, refer to page 136 for Border Instructions.

Putting It All Together

Trim the backing fabric and batting so they are 4-inches larger than the runner top. Refer to Finishing the Quilt on page 135 for complete instructions.

Binding
Cutting
From RED PRINT:

- Cut 4, 2-3/4 x 42-inch strips

Sew the binding to the quilt using a 3/8-inch seam allowance. This measurement will produce a 1/2-inch wide finished double binding. Refer to page 136 for Binding and Diagonal Piecing Instructions.

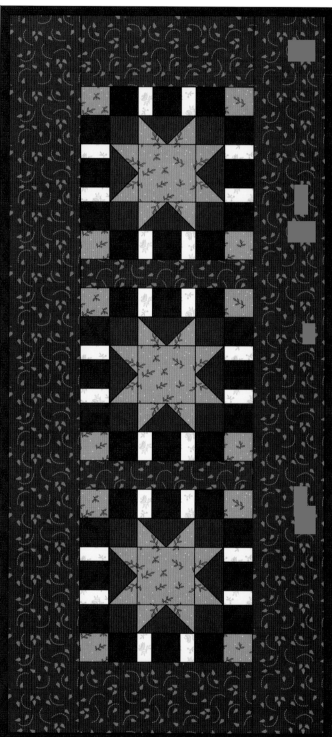

Picnic Table Runner

Pecan Biscotti

2-1/2 cups flour

1-1/2 tsp. baking powder

1/2 tsp. salt

1 tsp. ground cinnamon

1/2 cup unsalted butter at room temperature

1 cup sugar

3 eggs

1 T. vanilla

1/2 tsp. almond extract

2 cups toasted pecans, coarsely chopped

Preheat oven to 325 degrees. Stir together the flour, baking powder, salt and cinnamon. Set aside. In another bowl, combine butter and sugar using an electric mixer. Beat until light and fluffy. Add eggs one at a time, beating well after each one. Beat in vanilla and almond extracts.

Stir in the flour mixture, beating in one-third at a time at low speed. Fold in nuts.

Divide dough in half and place on a floured work surface. Roll each half into an oval log about 1-1/2" in diameter and 12" long. Place 1/2" apart on an ungreased baking sheet.

Bake about 30 minutes or until golden brown. Remove from oven and let cool until comfortable to touch.

Reduce oven temperature to 250 degrees.

Cut each log on the diagonal into slices 1" thick. Place slices, cut side down on the ungreased baking sheet and return to oven. Bake until lightly toasted and the edges are golden brown (about 10 minutes). Let cool.

Can be made 3 to 5 days in advance of serving and stored in an airtight container. If they do soften, recrisp by placing them in a 250 degree oven.

Makes 20–24 pieces.

Chicken or Turkey Salad

1, 7 oz. pkg. macaroni rings or shells

3 cups cooked chicken or turkey, cubed

1 cup grated carrots

1 cup diced celery

1 medium onion, diced

1/2 cup each: sliced radishes, diced green pepper, green olives, and parsley

Dressing:

1-1/2 cups mayonnaise

1/4 cup lemon juice

1/3 cup sugar

1 tsp. salt

Dash of pepper

Cook macaroni according to package instructions. Mix dressing ingredients; pour over the macaroni, chicken and vegetables; mix well.

Makes 8 servings.

celebrate with winning recipes
Game Day

GAME DAY
PARTY

ST. OLAF
vs.
ST. THOMAS

After the Game!   Trevor and Kerry's Place
                                   2724 Webster Ave. S., St. Louis Park
Saturday, October 14

Catch the flavor of the day. "Football fever" often heralds the onset of autumn and you can treat your favorite armchair quarterbacks to a fantastic game day menu that's easy to prepare long before the first kick-off. Your fans will appreciate helping themselves to a Focaccia sandwich divided into generous portions, along with raisin cookies and crisp apples. Country-cottage style decorating calls for combining rich earthy flavors of food with colors of the same in the flowers, serving pieces, and handsome plaid napkins. The stacked and inverted bowls and pottery pie plates vary the height of serving dishes and add interest to the buffet setting.

Game Day
Invitations

Make the perfect catch. You'll score big with this football invitation cut from folded corrigated cardboard (available at most craft stores). Type up the game day invitation sized to fit the football shape and glue it to the inside. On the front, draw the seam line of the football with a black marking pen and use a white shoelace for the lacing.

Make an extra invitation to use as a centerpiece for the game day buffet table. The invitation shown below is paired with a vintage football and an autumn bouquet arranged in a discarded Bean Pot that was put out of commission when a restaurant was remodeled in 1950.

Autumn Hues

When planning a color scheme for game day or any other autumn celebration, turn to nature for your inspiration. Even the tradition of bobbing for apples which inspired the copper canner filled with floating apple and pumpkin candles shown on page 113, is thought to have originated with an ancient Roman autumn festival honoring Pomona, the goddess of fruit.

Focaccia Sandwich

1 loaf Focaccia bread

8 oz. sliced ham

8 oz. sliced smoked turkey

4 oz. hard salami

2 T. olive oil

1 onion, sliced

1 tomato, sliced

1 lb. provalone cheese

Slice bread in half, horizontally. Sauté onion in olive oil and place on bottom half of bread. Layer remaining ingredients, ending with cheese and tomatoes. Place top half of bread on layered meats, cheese and tomato.

Wrap in foil and bake at 325 degrees for 20 to 30 minutes.

Cut loaf into 8 wedges Serve warm.

Makes 8 servings.

Raisin Cookies

1 cup sugar

1 cup shortening

1 cup raisins

5 tsp. raisin juice

2 eggs

1-1/2 cups oatmeal

1-1/2 cups flour

1 tsp. soda

1 tsp. cinnamon

1 tsp. cloves

chopped walnuts (optional)

Add 1 cup boiling water to raisins to soften and plump up. Let stand while creaming sugar and shortening.

Drain water off, reserving 5 tsp. raisin juice. Add raisins, juice, eggs and oatmeal to sugar and shortening.

Blend soda, cloves, and cinnamon with the flour and add to mixture. Stir in chopped walnuts. Drop by rounded teaspoons onto greased cookie sheet.

Bake for 8 to 11 minutes at 375 degrees.

Makes 48 cookies.

kid friendly and crowd pleasing
Pumpkin Carving Time

Celebrate an old Celtic custom. Because the Celtic year ended with the harvest, families gathered to feast and give thanks for the bounty of harvested crops. To light the way to the feast, decorative lanterns made from large carved turnips were often hung outside homes and along pathways. Suitors visiting their sweethearts brought along treats to swap with the younger children for a few moments of privacy. When these Halloween traditions were brought to America by immigrants, jack-o'-lanterns replaced turnips and courting gave way to trick-or-treating.

Pumpkin Carving
Time

Join us for
Pumpkin Carving
& Sunday Night Supper

Date
Sunday, October 29

Time
5:00 p.m.

Place
Kerry & Trevor's

Pumpkin Carving
Invitations

Celebrate the mystery and magic. When the intense blue sky of late October contrasts with the fiery-hued last leaves of autumn, and pumpkins too numerous to count dot the fields of farms in the surrounding countryside, Halloween fun is just around the corner. Not just for kids, Halloween is a time to invite friends and family to a pumpkin carving party followed by a Sunday Night Supper worthy of any harvest feast.

Include both events on a Pumpkin Carving Time invitation printed on heavy paper, cut out using a novelty paper edger, and mounted on black corrugated paper (available from most craft stores). Insert the invitation into a fabric bag, shown opposite and on page 116, that can also be used for holding Halloween treats. To make the party treat bag, turn the page for instructions and patterns.

Collections

For small-scale decorating, fill a country cottage with antique collectible candles displayed in a doll cupboard such as the one shown above. Or, create the tiny tabletop display, below, using a lidless black cookie jar topped by a Jack Frost pumpkin which casts an eerie shadow by candlelight on the wall.

Pumpkin Carving Time

Join us for
Pumpkin Carving
& Sunday Night Supper

Date
Sunday, October 29

Time
5:00 p.m.

Place
Kerry & Trevor's

Party Treat Bag

This treat bag delivers! You can count on this quick-to-make treat bag to keep on delivering long after the invitation arrives. It's as simple as fusing pumpkin or leaf appliqués cut from Thimbleberries® fabrics in rich autumn colors onto a coordinating pumpkin print, which is then fused to the wrapping paper used for lining the bag. Insert the invitation to the pumpkin carving party into the finished bag which can be reused to hold Halloween treats. Make extra bags to use at the pumpkin carving party. Fill a huge bowl with candy, and watch as your delighted guests scoop the treats into their bags as a party-favor farewell.

$\mathcal{I}$nstructions

Party Treat Bag
Assembly

Appliqué shapes are at right.

Step 1   With a hot dry iron, fuse the 8-1/2 x 11-inch fusible web rectangle to the wrong side of the Medium Print rectangle. Let cool and peel away the paper backing. Position the fused fabric on the wrong side of the wrapping paper rectangle and, with a hot dry iron, fuse in place.

Step 2   Trim the fabric/wrapping paper rectangle to 7-1/2 x 10-inches using a pinking shears, novelty paper edger, or rotary pinking cutter.

Step 3   Fold the side edges of the rectangle to the back, overlapping them 1 inch. Crease the folded edges well. Using the 1/2 x 7-inch fusible web strip, fuse the overlapping edges together.

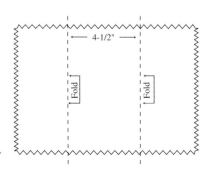

Step 4   Fold the bottom edge up 1/2-inch, crease the folded edge well, and machine-stitch to secure in place.

Step 5   Referring to Step 1, prepare the appliqué shapes and fuse them onto the gift bag.

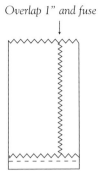

Overlap 1" and fuse

The appliqué pieces are reversed images for tracing onto fusible web.

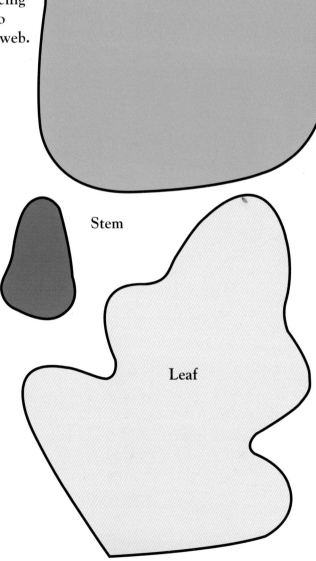

Pumpkin

Stem

Leaf

Pumpkin
Carving Party

Get inspired by Halloween history.

Antique and reproduction Halloween memorabilia provide more than grins for serious pumpkin carving. Kerry and Trevor find casual cottage-style entertaining easy-on-the-budget and a perfect crowd-pleaser for their friends from college. Below, the newspaper-topped picnic table comes indoors and a Log Cabin quilt adds warmth to the wall as well as hiding a basement window. Bottled root beer and orange soda complement the color scheme.

Carving Fun

Reviving childhood memories, Kerry and Trevor, above, discover that pumpkin carving can still be a lot of fun even for hardworking young professionals.

Several easy cut-outs for pumpkins such as the ones shown below are provided on the opposite page. Before the party, sharpen your carving skills on smaller pumpkins that serve as luminaries for the table and walkways and then graduate to a large tangle-toothed jack-o'-lantern. Fill it with a candle protected by a hurricane glass, and then nestle it inside a rustic grapevine wreath—a glowing tribute to the joys of Halloween.

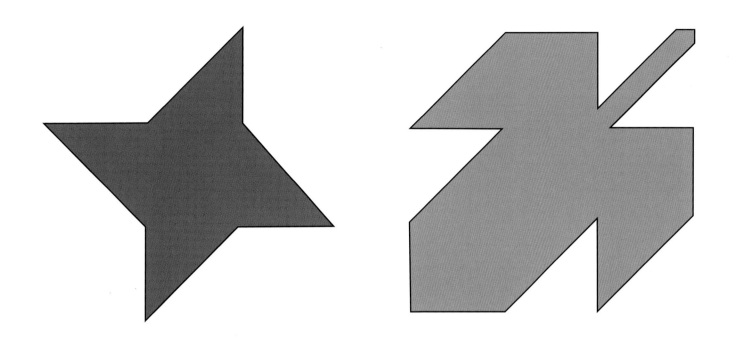

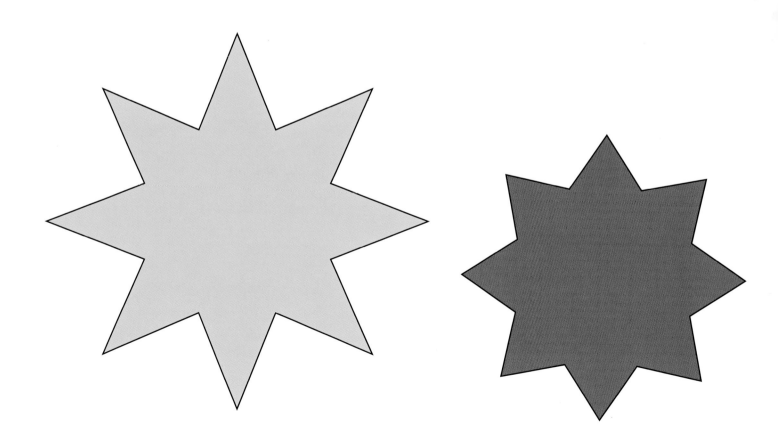

a hearty harvest feast
Sunday Night Supper

Build on tradition. Harvest suppers haven't changed much in the years since the ancient Celtics celebrated the gathering in of newly-harvested crops. Main recipe ingredients are hearty autumn favorites such as the harvest popcorn, wild rice soup, and caramel apple cake shown here. Serve it all in true country-cottage style on an antique black-and-cream wool blanket with a casual mix of table top decorations including a candle arrangement in an antique corn popper, a copper pail adding more warm tones, dried flowers in a paper-maché pumpkin, and a bouquet of autumn flowers to dress up the caramel apple cake resting on an inverted bowl for a special presentation.

Instructions

Add the finishing touches. Creating a clever place card holder to coordinate with the pumpkin patchwork napkin is as simple as placing a miniature pumpkin in a candy corn-filled ramekin. Copper wire, curled by wrapping it around a wooden spoon handle, holds the card.

Fabrics & Supplies

Finished Size: 16-inches square

Makes 4 napkins

Yardage is based on 42-inch wide fabric

16, 6 x 20-inch pieces of
ASSORTED DARK PRINTS for napkin tops

1 yard GREEN PRINT for napkin backs

Pumpkin Patchwork Napkins

Cutting

From ASSORTED DARK PRINTS:
- Cut 64, 4-1/2-inch squares

From GREEN PRINT:
- Cut 4, 16-1/2-inch squares

Piecing

Step 1   To make one napkin, use 16 of the 4-1/2-inch Dark Print squares. Sew the squares together in 4 rows of 4 squares each. Press the seam allowances in alternating directions by rows so the seams will fit snugly together with less bulk.

Step 2   Pin the rows at the block intersections, and sew the rows together. Press the seam allowances in one direction. At this point the napkin top should measure 16-1/2-inches square.

Step 3   With right sides together, layer the pieced napkin top and a 16-1/2-inch Green square. Sew the layers together 1/4-inch from the raw edges, leaving a 3-inch opening on one side for turning.

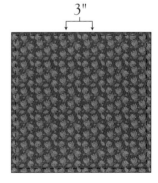

Step 4   Clip the corner seam allowances, turn the napkin right side out and press, taking care to see that the edges are sharp and even. Hand-stitch the opening closed.

Step 5   Machine-stitch in the ditch along the seam lines of the pieced napkin top.

Step 6   Repeat Steps 1 through 5 to make a total of 4 pieced napkins.

Wild Rice Soup

2 med. stalks celery, sliced

1 med. carrot, coarsely shredded

1 med. onion, chopped (about 1/2 cup)

1 small green pepper, chopped

2 T. margarine or butter

3 T. all-purpose flour

1 tsp. salt

1/4 tsp. pepper

1-1/2 cups cooked wild rice

2 cups chicken broth

1 cup whole cream

1/3 cup toasted slivered almonds

1/4 cup snipped parsley

4 slices thick, lean bacon, cooked and crumbled

Cook wild rice following package directions. Cook and stir celery, carrot, onion and green pepper in margarine in 3-quart saucepan until celery is tender (about 5 minutes). Stir in flour, salt and pepper. Add chicken broth slowly, stirring constantly to blend in flour. Add wild rice. Heat to boiling.

Cover and simmer, stirring occasionally, 15 minutes. Stir in cream, almonds, parsley and bacon. Heat just until hot, but do not boil.

Makes 5 servings, about 1 cup each.

Note: May add cooked, diced chicken for a heartier soup.

Harvest Popcorn

4 quarts popped corn

1, 9 oz. can shoestring potatoes

2 T. melted butter

1/2 tsp. garlic powder

1/2 tsp. dried dill

Mix popcorn and shoestring potatoes in large mixing bowl.

Combine butter, garlic powder and dill. Pour mixture over popcorn and toss to coat evenly.

Makes 6 servings.

Caramel Apple Cake

1-1/2 cups vegetable oil

3 eggs

2 cups sugar

2 tsp. vanilla

3 cups flour

1 tsp. soda

1 tsp. salt

1-1/2 cups chopped pecans

3 cups peeled, diced apples

Combine oil, eggs, sugar and vanilla. Mix until well blended. Combine flour, soda and salt and add to egg mixture. Beat with mixer until completely blended. Fold in apples and pecans. The batter will be quite stiff. Spoon batter into a well greased and floured bundt pan.

Bake at 350 degrees for 1 hour and 20 minutes. Leave cake in pan until completely cool, then invert onto cake plate. Top with caramel topping.

Makes 12–16 servings.

Caramel Topping

1/2 cup packed brown sugar

1/4 cup milk

1/2 cup butter

Mix and bring to a slow rolling boil. Cook for 3 minutes. Let sauce rest for 5 minutes. Drizzle over cake.

Salted Peanut Cookies

1 cup brown sugar

1 cup white sugar

1 cup shortening

2 eggs

1-1/2 tsp. vanilla

1 tsp. baking powder

1 tsp. baking soda

2 cups flour

1 cup corn flakes, well crushed

1 cup quick cooking oatmeal

1 cup salted Spanish peanuts

Cream together brown and white sugars with shortening. Beat eggs, and add to creamed mixture along with the vanilla.

Sift together flour, baking powder and soda and combine with creamed mixture. Stir in corn flakes, oatmeal, and peanuts. Roll into balls. Place on cookie sheet and flatten slightly.

Bake at 375 degrees for about 12 minutes.

Makes 48 cookies.

Harvest Table Runner

Make good use of the mellow warmth of brown. Setting a festive harvest table begins with a table runner rich with the earthy, inviting hues of brown. The no-sew runner shown here starts with bird, sunflower, leaf, and pumpkin appliqués fused to a brown rice paper rectangle finished with a dogtooth border cut from dark green rice paper. The enduring appeal of browns and golds is enhanced by a harvest potpourri of miniature Indian corn mixed with strawflower blossoms.

Instructions

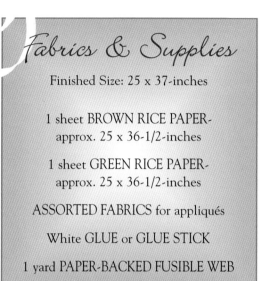

Fabrics & Supplies

Finished Size: 25 x 37-inches

1 sheet BROWN RICE PAPER-
approx. 25 x 36-1/2-inches

1 sheet GREEN RICE PAPER-
approx. 25 x 36-1/2-inches

ASSORTED FABRICS for appliqués

White GLUE or GLUE STICK

1 yard PAPER-BACKED FUSIBLE WEB

Table Runner

Assembly

Appliqué shapes are below and on page 126.

Step 1   Position the fusible web (paper side up) over the appliqué shapes. With a pencil trace the shapes the number of times indicated on each pattern, leaving a small margin between each shape. Cut the shapes apart.

Step 2   Following the manufacturer's instructions, fuse the shapes to the wrong side of the fabrics chosen for the appliqués. Let the fabric cool and cut along the traced line of each shape. Peel away the paper backing from the fusible web.

Step 3   Referring to the runner diagram, position the appliqué shapes on the brown rice paper, and fuse in place.

Step 4   Trace dogtooth border onto green rice paper. Cut 2 short strips for ends of the runner. Cut 2 long strips for the sides of the runner. Add a few extra inches on the ends to allow for adjustments. Overlap the green dogtooth border onto the brown runner 1/2-inch. Adjust strips so points meet at the corners. Glue borders onto runner with white glue or glue stick. Trim excess.

**The appliqué pieces
are reversed images
for tracing onto
fusible web.**

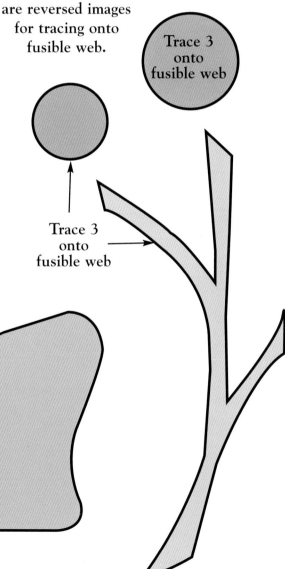

**Trace 3
onto
fusible web**

**Trace 3
onto
fusible web**

**Trace 3
onto
fusible web**

Trace 6
onto
fusible
web

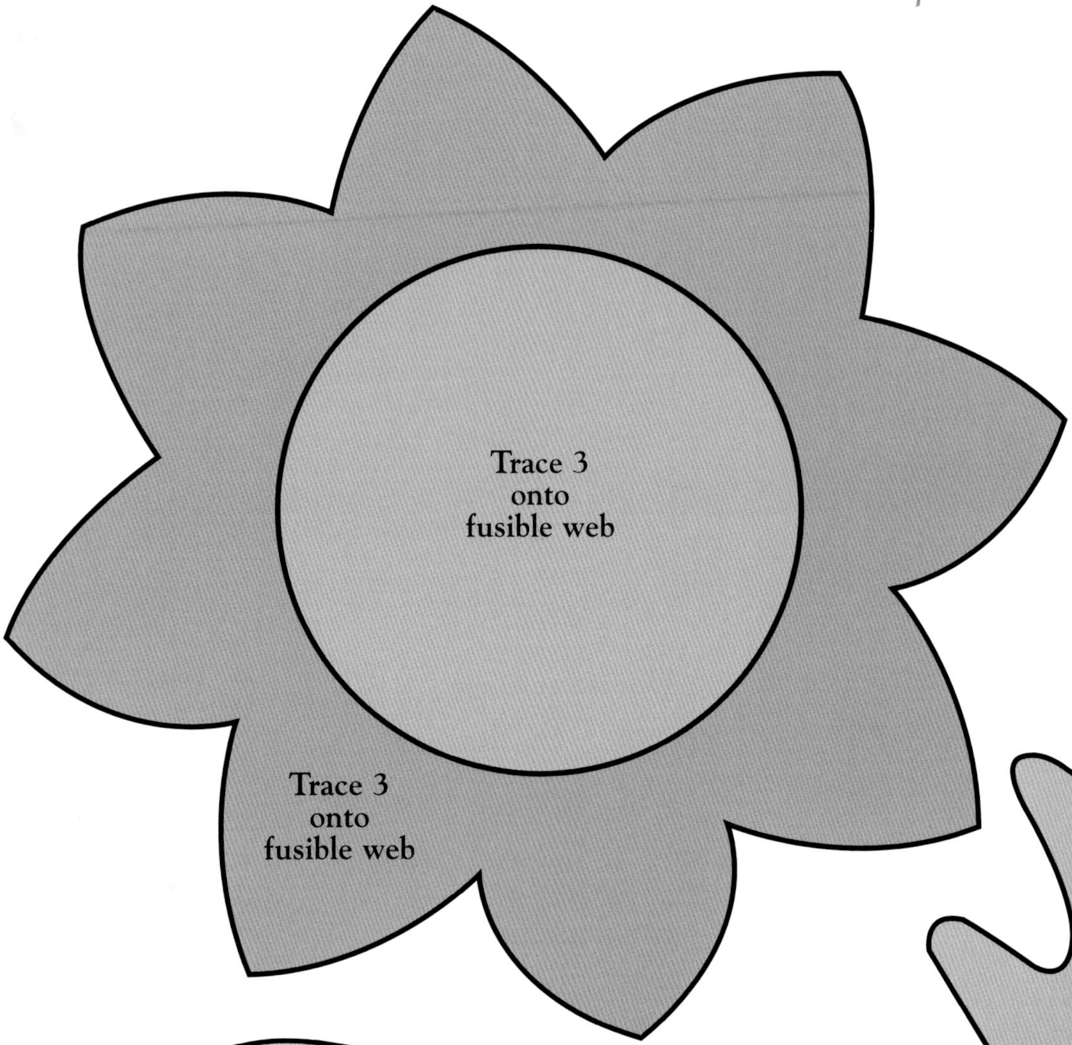

The appliqué
pieces are
reversed images
for tracing onto
fusible web.

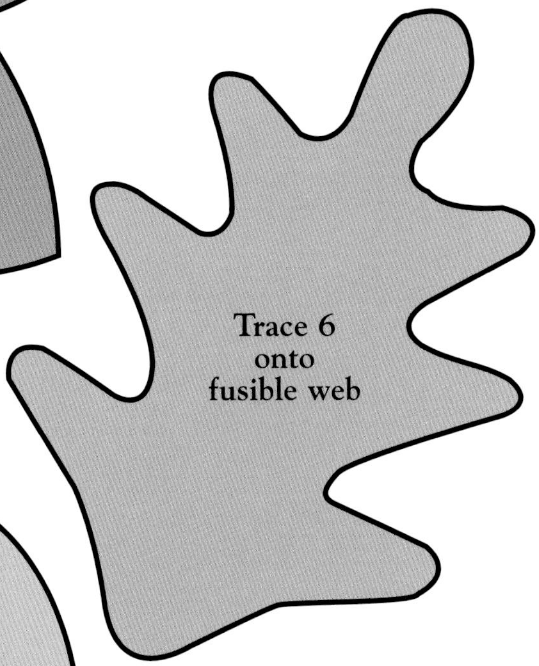

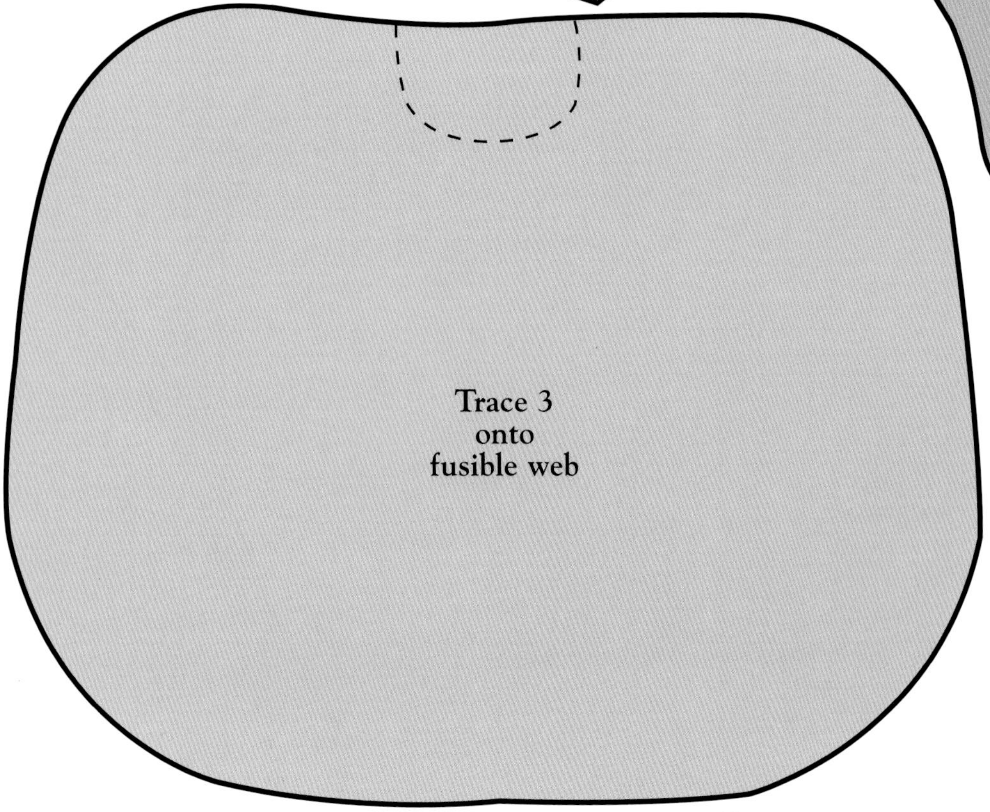

Trace 3
onto
fusible web

Trace 3
onto
fusible web

Trace 6
onto
fusible web

Trace 3
onto
fusible web

Trace 3
onto
fusible
web

Harvest Table Runner

Dogtooth Border Pattern

Repeat as needed

Harvest Table Runner

comfort and joy
Christmas Brunch

Serve up hearty helpings of hospitality. Informality is the secret to holiday entertaining infused with country-cottage spirit. On Christmas Day, rising to the occasion should be stress-free and fun for you as well as your guests. Extend glad tidings to all with oven-baked French toast and a quick holiday egg scramble served up on pine cone pottery and a patchwork tablecloth. For more about the gift box party favor, please turn the page.

Holiday Egg Scramble

2 T. vegetable oil

2 T. butter

1 small green pepper, finely chopped

1 bunch green onions, sliced

1 cup finely sliced ham, cut into 1/4" wide strips (5-1/2 ozs.)

4 oz. mushrooms, sliced (1-1/2 cups)

1 lb. 4 oz. package of cooked, sliced home fries

10 beaten eggs

1/4 cup milk

1/4 tsp. salt

1/8 tsp. pepper

1 cup shredded cheddar cheese (4 oz.)

In a 15-inch non-stick skillet, sauté the green pepper, onion, ham and mushrooms in the oil over medium-high heat until soft, stirring occasionally. Cook until the moisture from the mushrooms has evaporated. Set aside.

Add the butter to the same skillet, then the cooked potatoes. Cook and stir occasionally for 8 to 10 minutes or until potatoes are slightly browned.

Combine eggs, milk, salt and pepper. Add to skillet. Reduce heat to medium and cook, stirring occasionally until eggs are just set. Add pepper, onion, ham, and mushroom mixture.

Sprinkle with cheese. Cover and cook without stirring for 3 minutes.

Makes 8–10 servings.

Oven French Toast

3 beaten eggs

1-1/2 cups milk

3 T. sugar

1/2 tsp. vanilla

8 slices 1" thick French bread

3 T. butter or margarine

Cinnamon and sugar mixture

1/2 cup chopped pecans

Mix first four ingredients. Melt butter and pour evenly on bottom of cookie sheet. Soak 8 pieces bread, one at a time, in the mixture and place on cookie sheet. Bake at 350 degrees for 15 minutes. Turn bread over and sprinkle with mixture of cinnamon and sugar. Bake an additional 10 minutes or until golden brown. Sprinkle with chopped pecans and maple syrup.

Makes 4 servings.

Party Favor

Create cottage style comfort—naturally! The gift box party favor shown below can also be used as a place card by adding the guest's name to the star-stenciled slice of pine. To decorate the miniature lidded paper-maché box, begin by painting it deep red and adding white dots of paint applied with the handled end of a small paint brush. Stencil a star in the center of a thin "slice" or round cut from the base of a cleverly recycled Christmas tree. Drill a tiny hole in the tree round and use a piece of wire to tie it tightly to the curling ribbon bow so it stands upright.

For the Christmas brunch tabletop, continue the natural theme by cutting logs into 2-inch thick rounds. Stack several log rounds to use as a base for a glass-shaded candle, as shown below right.

Christmas Brunch

Date
Saturday, December 16

Time
11:00 a.m.

Place
2724 Webster Avenue South
St. Louis Park

Hostess
Kerry & Trevor

You're Invited

Inviting ideas for a memorable cottage-style Christmas brunch begin with the festive invitation shown above. Printed on vellum purchased at a stationery store, the invitation is held in place with old-fashioned gold picture corners. A simple pine bough rubber stamp was used to create an all-over pattern for the cover stock background.

When guests arrive, treat them to an inviting outdoor accessory—a sleigh filled with greens and a red wooden bowl brimming with boughs, cones, and apples surrounding a single candle—the season's symbol of warmth and good cheer.

general Instructions

general
Instructions

Getting Started

- Yardage is based on 42"-wide fabric.

- A rotary cutter, mat, and wide clear plastic ruler with 1/8" markings are needed tools in attaining accuracy. A 6" x 24" ruler is recommended.

- Read instructions thoroughly before beginning project.

- Prewash and press fabrics.

- Place right sides of fabric pieces together and use 1/4" seam allowances throughout unless otherwise specified.

- Seam allowances are included in the cutting sizes given. It is very important that accurate 1/4" seam allowances are used. It is wise to stitch a sample 1/4" seam allowance to check your machine's seam allowance accuracy.

- Press seam allowances toward the darker fabric and/or in the direction that will create the least amount of bulk.

Hints and Helps from Lynette for: Pressing Strip Sets

When sewing strips of fabric together for strip sets, it is important to press the seam allowances nice and flat, usually to the darker fabric. Be careful not to stretch as you press, causing a "rainbow effect." This will affect the accuracy and shape of the pieces cut from the strip set. I like to press on the wrong side first and with the strips perpendicular to the ironing board. Then I flip the piece over and press on the right side to prevent little pleats from forming at the seams. Laying the strip set lengthwise on the ironing board seems to encourage the rainbow effect, as shown in diagram.

Avoid this rainbow effect

Borders

Note: Cut borders to the width called for. Always cut border strips a few inches longer than needed, just to be safe. Diagonally piece the border strips together as needed.

Step 1 With pins, mark the center points along all 4 sides of the quilt. For the top and bottom borders measure the quilt from left to right through the middle.

Step 2 Measure and mark the border lengths and center points on the strips cut for the borders before sewing them on.

Step 3 Pin the border strips to the quilt and stitch a 1/4" seam. Press the seam allowances toward the borders. Trim off excess border lengths.

Trim away excess fabric

Step 4 For the side borders, measure your quilt from top to bottom, including the borders just added, to determine the length of the side borders.

Step 5 Measure and mark the side border lengths as you did for the top and bottom borders.

Step 6 Pin and stitch the side border strips in place. Press and trim the border strips even with the borders just added.

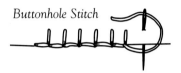

Trim away excess fabric

Step 7 If your quilt has multiple borders, measure, mark, and sew additional borders to the quilt in the same manner.

Decorative Stitches

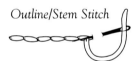

Buttonhole Stitch

Outline/Stem Stitch

Straight Stitch

Finishing the Quilt

Step 1 Remove the selvages from the backing fabric. Sew the long edges together, and press. Trim the backing and batting so they are 2" to 4" larger than the quilt top.

Step 2 Mark the quilt top for quilting. Layer the backing, batting, and quilt top. Baste the 3 layers together and quilt.

Step 3 When quilting is complete, remove basting. Baste all 3 layers together a scant 1/4" from the edge. This hand-basting keeps the layers from shifting and prevents puckers from forming when adding the binding. Trim excess batting and backing fabric even with the edge of the quilt top. Add the binding as shown on page 136.

Binding and Diagonal Piecing

Diagonal Piecing

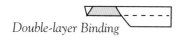

Stitch
diagonally

Trim to 1/4"
seam
allowance

Press seam
open

Step 1 Diagonally piece the binding strips. Fold the strip in half lengthwise, wrong sides together, and press.

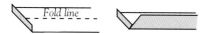

Double-layer Binding

Step 2 Unfold and trim one end at a 45° angle. Turn under the edge 1/4" and press. Refold the strip.

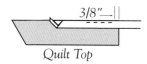

Fold line

Step 3 With raw edges of the binding and quilt top even, stitch with a 3/8" seam allowance, starting 2" from the angled end.

Step 4 Miter the binding at the corners. As you approach a corner of the quilt, stop sewing 3/8" from the corner of the quilt.

3/8"

Quilt Top

Step 5 Clip the threads and remove the quilt from under the presser foot.

Step 6 Flip the binding strip up and away from the quilt, then fold the binding down even with the raw edge of the quilt. Begin sewing at the upper edge. Miter all 4 corners in this manner.

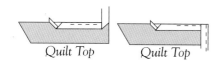

Quilt Top   *Quilt Top*

Step 7 Trim the end of the binding so it can be tucked inside of the beginning binding about 3/8". Finish stitching the seam.

Quilt Back   *Quilt Back*

Step 8 Turn the folded edge of the binding over the raw edges and to the back of the quilt so that the stitching line does not show. Hand-sew the binding in place, folding in the mitered corners as you stitch.

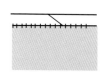

Quilt Back   *Quilt Back*   *Quilt Back*

Trimming Side and Corner Triangles

- Begin at a corner by lining up your ruler 1/4-inch beyond the points of the corners of the blocks as shown. Draw a light line along the edge of the ruler. Repeat this procedure on all four sides of the quilt top, lightly marking cutting lines.

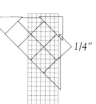
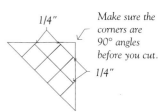

1/4"

Mark cutting lines lightly 1/4" beyond the points of the corners of the blocks.

1/4"

Make sure the corners are 90° angles before you cut.

1/4"

- Check all the corners before you do any cutting. Adjust the cutting lines as needed to ensure square corners.

- When you are certain that everything is as square as it can be, position your ruler over the quilt top. Using your marked lines as guides, cut away the excess fabric with your rotary cutter, leaving a 1/4-inch seam allowance beyond the block corners.

Making Yo-Yos

Step 1   Trace a 3-inch diameter circle onto template material for the yo-yo and cut it out.

Step 2   Trace around the template on the wrong side of the fabric squares.

Step 3   Turn the edges of each circle under 1/8-inch, judging this distance by eye. Take care to keep the seam allowances of each circle the same size. Use one strand of quilting thread to make running stitches close to the fold. Make these stitches approximately 1/4-inch long and 1/4-inch apart.

Step 4   To form each yo-yo, pull up the gathering thread so that the circle is gathered on the right side. Take a few stitches through the gathered folds and knot the thread. Clip the threads close to the fabric. The back side of the yo-yo will be flat.

Step 5   Stitch the yo-yos together with fine whip stitches at the outer edges. To do so, place the yo-yos right sides together and whip-stitch about a 1/8-inch section. Make a secure knot and clip the thread. Continue adding yo-yos in this fashion.

Step 6   Stitch yo-yos together in rows.

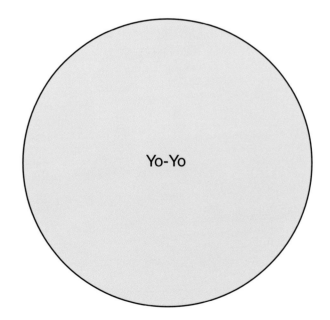

Yo-Yo

Quilt Sources

Lynette Jensen's designs for the quilts and decorative accessories featured in COTTAGE COMFORT are available from her Thimbleberries® line of books and patterns, or from Rodale Press Please call 800/587-3944 to order a catalog, or for more information about obtaining patterns for the quilts and tablecloth shown below.

Grandmother's Flower Garden Quilt
(Personal Antique Collection) **10**

Yo-Yo Quilt
(Personal Antique Collection) **20**

Cottage Flower Quilt
(The Thimbleberries® Book of Quilts) **22**

Meadow Lily Quilt
(At Home with Thimbleberries® Quilts) **44**

Christmas Patches Tablecloth
(Thimbleberries® Holiday Collection) **128**

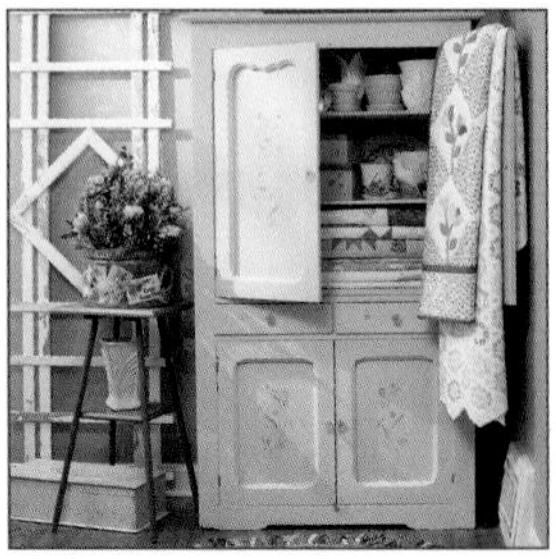

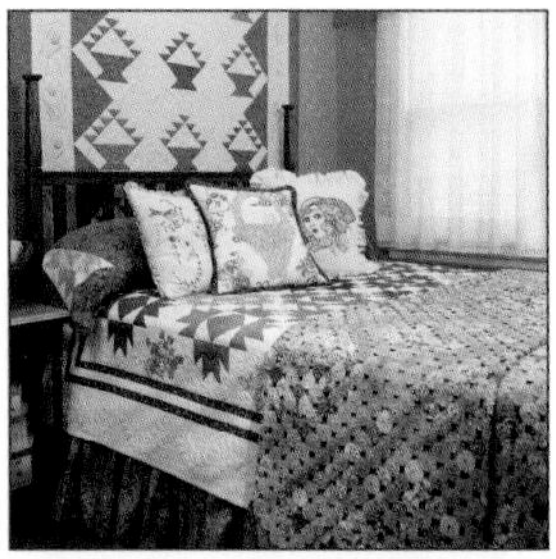

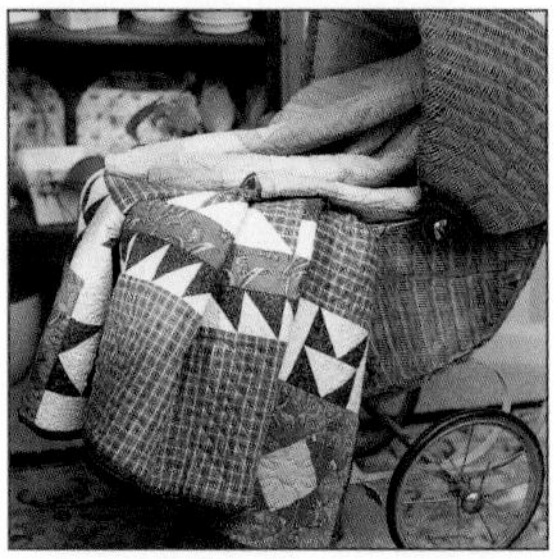

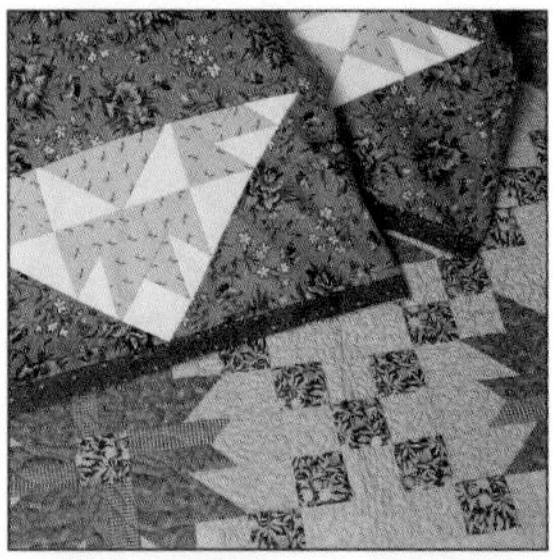

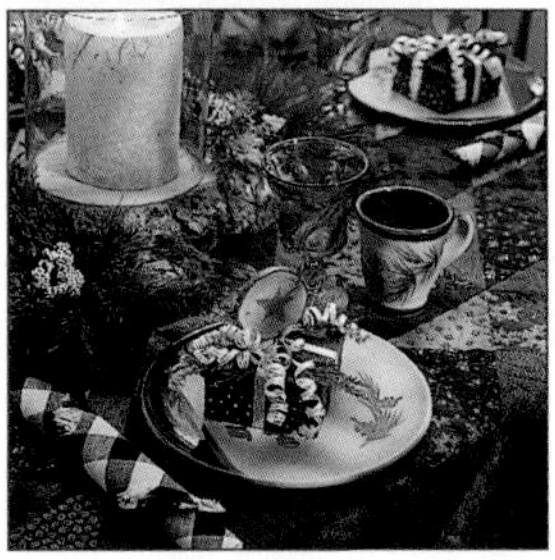

Decorative Sources

Project Index

Recipe Index